The Garden Equation

How to turn your garden into a
delightful part of your lifestyle

SALLY TIERNEY

Second paperback edition printed 2015 in the United Kingdom.

A catalogue record is available from the British Library.

Published by Foxrock Publications

For more copies of this book, please email :

sally@yorkshiregardendesigner.co.uk

Tel: +44 (0)1904 623 343

Illustrations by Ella Tierney and Rory Sheard

Designed and Set by www.bookstyle.co.uk

ISBN: 978-0-9934521-1-6

I dedicate this book to my husband and children
for their love, support and patience.

Contents

Introduction

Every gardener dreams of having a delightful garden. I know this is true: every year hundreds of thousands of people, just like you, visit gardens for pleasure up and down the country. Yet in reality, the garden at home is often seen as an encumbrance that takes up too much of your time and energy. Keeping on top of it becomes something you are unable, or unwilling to put the necessary time into, because you have other commitments - work, travelling, caring for the family, or enjoying retirement.

Perhaps you know all too well how that feels?

What is really happening is that your garden is out of tune with you and your lifestyle. By this I mean that your garden requires more time to look after than you have available. This situation occurs quite often, and it does not come from a lack of effort, enthusiasm, or horticultural expertise. I've spoken to some very knowledgeable gardeners over the years who have found themselves at their wits' end, because they think the garden is just too big to cope with, or they do not have enough time to keep it tidy.

I believe, based on eighteen years experience as a professional garden designer, that this happens because you have not based your garden on the Three Foundation Steps that make up The Garden Equation.

The Garden Equation consists of three steps which, if used and applied correctly, will enable you to make the right choices about time and maintenance to create the ideal garden to fit in with you and your lifestyle. Hopefully, by the end of this book, you will be thinking about the garden as an integral and essential part of your immediate living space, one that is just as important to you as a room in your home.

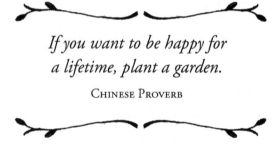

*If you want to be happy for
a lifetime, plant a garden.*

Chinese Proverb

Step One: The Experience of the Garden

Know exactly what you want to have, or do, in your garden. What is it that makes being outside in the garden an enjoyable experience for you?

Step Two: The Physical Conditions

Identify and use the physical conditions in the garden that are already present, and use plants that will thrive there. Work with nature, not against it.

Step Three: Maintenance Considerations

Assess the maintenance implications of the design *before* the garden is built. If necessary, tailor the plan while it is still on paper or your existing garden, to make sure that the maintenance fits in with the time you have.

Benefits of Using the Three Foundation Steps

By adapting the way you think about the garden, and basing all the decisions you make about your outdoor living space on the Three Foundation Steps, your garden will always be a source of delight, regardless of the day you have had, or the circumstances you are dealing with. There are, however, all sorts of additional benefits that you won't have anticipated, which often only become apparent once the garden has been designed/adapted, built, and planted. One client told me his social life had doubled because he finally had a space he could entertain in, while another said she had more time and energy to enjoy being with her grandchild. Others have told me that they feel excited and relieved that the garden is, at last, manageable. The one aspect that the majority of past clients have spoken of, however, is the freedom they have experienced, being able to simply enjoy spending time in their garden without any pressure.

It is not necessary to have a lot of horticultural experience to use The Garden Equation. You do, however, require the desire to have a lovely, enjoyable garden!

What This Book Is
The Garden Equation is a practical guide for applying my signature method of foundation garden design to your own garden, be it an existing garden, or a new one you are starting from scratch. To make *the book* as user-friendly as possible I have divided it into two parts:

Part One: Making a Start on Your Garden
This section is about how to get the right information. The Garden Equation process will allow you to make informed decisions about your garden in the future. In this section of the book you will learn:

- Each of the Three Foundation Steps in detail
- How to apply each Foundation Step
- Why each Foundation Step is important, with some case studies provided to illustrate the points made
- Where to find ideas and inspiration
- The implications of your design choices in relation to maintenance
- How to avoid the most common mistakes people make
- The next steps, and what options you have

Part Two: Ensuring Your Garden Stays Enjoyable in the Future

In the second section I will show you how to use the same Garden Equation process to adapt your garden when something life-changing happens that affects how and when you use the garden. Examples of the types of changes I mean would be a new job, caring for a relative, or adapting to an illness.

What This Book IS NOT

This is not a book about how to design your own garden, how to create a planting plan, or a guide to specific gardening techniques.

How Do I Know This Book Works?

The Garden Equation has been tried, tested, and modified over the past eighteen years, not just in my own garden, but in many of the gardens that have been designed by my company, Yorkshire Garden Designer. Not only have I seen the long-term successes of gardens that have been solidly based on the Three Foundation Steps, I've also seen gardens where those steps have been missed out, or skimped on, resulting in the gardens becoming a burden on their owners.

In my experience, when a garden has been built on the foundations of The Garden Equation it will always be a pleasure to look after, because it evolves with you, as and when your lifestyle changes. For the unavoidable maintenance that you really do not enjoy, you can take encouragement from the fact that you are doing a particular task as a means to an end - a very specific end, because you have already identified it as important to you in Step One.

As a result of using The Garden Equation and adapting your thinking, I know that your garden will become a seamless and integral part of your lifestyle, beyond your hopes and expectations, so let's get going!

Part One

Chapter 1

What Is Preventing Your Garden Being a Delight

If you have picked up this book, and got this far in, I'm betting you feel pretty frustrated with your garden? You might also be feeling embarrassed, either by your garden itself, or your inability to do something about it. Here are two observations that will help you change things:

- In my experience, the majority of garden owners are in the same boat as you. You are by no means alone in your exasperation!
- Over the past eighteen years I have noticed the same types of problems that crop up time and again, regardless of the size of the garden, the budget, or the degree of enthusiasm and/or knowledge of the gardener.

See if any of these **Common Problems** are familiar to you:

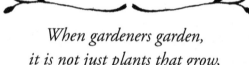 *You Do not Know Where to Start*
Not knowing where to start is the most frequently encountered problem people talk to me about. It is crushing to know that you want to do something with your garden, but you have no idea how to begin transforming your unattractive garden into a place you would like to spend time.

The main reason you do not know where to start

When gardeners garden,
it is not just plants that grow,
but the gardeners themselves.

Ken Druse

is probably that you are not clear about what you would like to achieve in the garden.

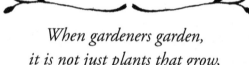 *You Do not Have Any Ideas*
When you are familiar and/or dissatisfied with a place, it is very difficult to be objective about it, making it almost impossible to come up with

fresh ideas. Without the right ideas, there is no way of working out what the first step should be.

The Physical State of the Garden Is Off-Putting

The physical state of the existing garden itself is also likely to be having an effect on you. You need to take this into account as it will be bringing up a whole host of negative emotions, and because you do not understand what is going on, you become very hesitant to act. Listed below are seven of the most frequently encountered situations you might be facing:

- **The Garden is a Mess**

  The garden is an overgrown mess, and you keep putting off getting to grips with it, until the problem becomes overwhelming. Eventually there comes a point when the task has become too big and you give up entirely - it doesn't take much to reach the tipping point.

- **The Garden is a Completely Empty Space**

  There is nothing more off-putting than an open space that doesn't have a purpose, even if that space is relatively small and enclosed, with definite boundaries. The reason for this is that you do not know what to do with yourself within the space, because there are no clues to help you. I believe this problem occurs because you become overwhelmed by your garden's potential and possibility because there are too many decisions to make. When you are in the garden it feels very uncomfortable, exposed and vulnerable, because there is nothing you can make sense of or anchor yourself with.

You may think that this sounds odd, especially if you enjoy being out in the wide open countryside, like the North York Moors, but when you think about it, all land has a definable purpose, whether it's accessible to the public or not. Most of the land is used for agriculture, something which we understand well. Elsewhere the definition would be preservation of a particular habitat or landscape, or somewhere people live and work. Even derelict land has a definition. I cannot think of any space in this country which does not have an obvious purpose.

In brief, you will feel uncomfortable and disconnected from any space that has no apparent purpose, which lacks *meaning*.

- **The Garden Space Has Been Changed**
  This will have happened either because you have extended your home, or you have bought more land and extended your garden. Now you have got part of a garden that you know well, and part that you do not. When this happens it is often

very difficult to see past the boundaries that you are familiar with in order to see the potential of the new space.

- **Someone Else's Style is Overwhelming**
  The garden has been designed in someone else's style, that is not yours. I once saw a new garden that could have been air-lifted from Morocco. The garden had been designed around a beautiful, hand-made, tiled water feature. The clients had travelled to Marrakesh, specifically to get it made, and then shipped it to the UK. The garden was stunning, in my opinion, but how would it be if you didn't like it, or you felt it was too-high maintenance? It was easy to see the quality of the materials used and the high standard of the workmanship. This would only make it harder to reach the very difficult decision that the garden was not the right one for your lifestyle. Getting past someone else's style isn't always easy.

- **You Are Forced to Accommodate an Issue**
  Sometimes you buy a garden that has something in it you must keep, as removing it would result in a fine and legal action. The most common issue of this nature are mature trees that are protected from being removed by a Tree Preservation Order (TPO). There are other legal designations to be aware of too, such as Conservation Areas,

National Parks, and Sites of Special Scientific Interest. When there is something that you have no choice over, it is often all too easy to just focus on the problem, making it difficult to see the rest of the garden.

A garden I am currently designing has two large mature sycamore trees in it, which are protected by a TPO. The clients would have to apply to the council if they want to remove so much as a branch, even if the branch is clearly unsafe. The trees are totally out of proportion with the size of the garden they are in, and their combined canopy covers ¾ of the garden in shade. They are completely inappropriate for the site, yet they are protected because they are part of an old avenue of trees that lined the driveway to the (now non-existent) vicarage. Clearly those particular trees would never have been planted if the planting had been designed to be sympathetic to the existing house.

- **The Garden looks Nice, But Doesn't Feel Right, and You Do not Know Why**
  This may sound odd, but you need your garden to feel like a garden should, to you. If your garden doesn't feel right it is impossible to relate to it or enjoy it. This is quite an ambiguous statement, but stop for a few minutes and think

about how your garden actually *feels* to you, not on an intellectual level, but at an instinctive one. Put another way, what is your *gut feeling* about your garden?

If you have no idea what I'm talking about, or even if you do, the next time you have half an hour and the weather is nice, go out into your garden and sit down in your favourite place. Make yourself comfortable, and then consider how the experience - albeit a small one - of simply sitting in your garden makes you feel. The crucial question to ask yourself is, 'Do I feel at ease sitting here?' or, put another way, 'Does this space feel right?'

I'm pretty certain that once you begin to consider things from this perspective, you will immediately know the answer. If the garden does not feel right to you, your actions will have spoken louder than any words, in that you will have found all sorts of reasons to avoid going outside.

At a subconscious level you are instinctively responding to the structure and ordering of the space. If it is on a scale that you can relate to - which is usually determined by where you grew up, or by your previous experiences of the outdoors - and it has an easily identifiable purpose, flow, and unity to it, then your sub-conscious recognises its form and is comfortable with it. Most people are unaware that these 'decisions' are being made all the time. You recognise the signals given by your sub-conscious when it feels 'safe' enough to enable your conscious self to let your guard down. Without analysing this too much, you will experience a connection, sense of comfort, and rightness about the space, which will convince you that the garden feels like a garden should - according to you and your personal criteria of needs. Amazingly, all this happens in less than a second.

This is not a unique experience to gardens, as you carry out this type of assessment on all the spaces you inhabit or pass through. Now you know what is happening, I'm sure you can identify other occasions when you have, or have not, felt comfortable in a place.

- **You Can't Relate to the Garden**
  The garden is too big and you feel uncomfortable in it.

Within your sub-conscious is embedded a sense of scale and proportion, which developed during your childhood, and is loosely based on the types of landscapes you saw on a regular basis. Everything is measured against this internal scale and if the space is too big you will feel very exposed or vulnerable.

Alternatively the garden is too small and you feel claustrophobic in it.

You might be wondering what to do if your garden is too small for you, and you do not feel at home in it. Unfortunately you can't do anything to change the size but I'm certain you would not have bought the property in the first place unless there were compelling reasons beyond the garden.

You have Wasted Money on Plants That Look Terrible, or Died

I often see gardens whose owners haven't understood how important it is to identify the conditions of their specific garden, in order to make sure that the plants they buy will survive, and thrive. They have gone to the garden centre, enthusiastic to get going, and bought the first plant that caught their eye without checking that it was suitable for the conditions of their garden. Unfortunately, when this happens, the plant will still do what it has evolved to do, regardless of what the person buying it hopes it will do. A lot of money and dreams are wasted in this way.

I'll give you an example, albeit an extreme one.

I went to see a garden on a hillside in West York-shire. I thought it was very windy at the time, but to the owners it was a normal day. We talked about their garden, but regardless of what they wanted to have - which was swathes of colourful perennials - they had no choice but to accept that only plants that could survive the windy conditions would do well there. That meant grasses and other plants with long thin leaves.

Another example is lavender, which is one of the most popular plants in this country. It is a fact that this plant needs to be planted in a free drain-ing soil. It does not like its roots to be waterlogged in any way and when it encounters conditions it doesn't like, it dies - quite quickly, too. There is nothing you can do to change that, except to change the conditions in which the plant is planted. This is expensive and time consuming, and only a short term solution. The other option is to buy a different plant that *does* likes the condi-tions you have. This is a cheaper, faster, long-term solution. Which is easier to achieve?

Millions of pounds have been wasted and much pleasure ruined as a result of people failing to understand the implications of the conditions in their gardens, and failing to buy the right plants for the conditions they have.

The Garden Has Become a Burden

When a garden has become a burden in the eyes of its owner it is usually due to two main reasons:

One: The majority of garden owners I meet only think of maintenance as an afterthought. Maintenance is one of those things that must be done right from the beginning of a new garden, so that you can keep on top of it easily, with minimum effort. It is a much-made mistake to sit back and relax, because in the meantime weeds start to pop up, and become established before you know it - especially in the spring time. If maintenance is ignored, the time required to get the garden back to an acceptable state gets more and more, until the task has become impossible to achieve in the time you have got.

I have a client who spends ten minutes in his garden every evening after work. He has a glass of wine in his hand and he drinks this as he goes round with a hoe or trowel, rooting out any 'invaders', as he calls the weeds, and this is not a bad approach to have.

Two: The other reason the garden becomes a burden is a result of how the garden owner thinks of it in general. The home is the main living space and receives the most attention, whereas the garden is seen as just an add-on, usually with no purpose. With this approach, it is small wonder that the garden has become a burden!

What is a weed? A plant whose virtues have never been discovered.

RALPH WALDO EMERSON

The Garden is Approached in the Same Way as the Home

A very logical approach, often taken, is to tackle the garden in the same way as the home, where it's usually straightforward to establish the start point and make decisions based on the desired outcome. This is because you know a reasonable amount about your home and what you are trying to achieve. You are so used to doing it, automatically, that you are unaware of the processes you are going through. If you decide to put in a new bathroom suite, you know what's involved, where to go, and the outcome you want. Even if you have to do some research before making your mind up, you already know some of the deciding factors, such as size, colour, brand, and your budget.

Although the same decision-making process does also apply to creating a garden, you need additional information before you can begin to make sensible, realistic, and long-term decisions about your outside space. There are many people who do not know what information is required. If you do not know what sort of lifestyle you want outside, what the maintenance implications of those choices are, and what the existing growing conditions are, then you will never be able to create a realistic start point. People often conclude, once they start giving the garden some serious thought, that they do not know what they want to achieve. They then make no start, because they do not know what the desired outcome is and therefore do not know how to get going.

People Rush into Details Before Establishing the Big Picture

I've noticed that when garden owners do not know where to start, they often focus on details of secondary importance such as the garden furniture. In their enthusiasm to get going, the owners go out and buy all sorts of 'stuff' which often turns out to be superfluous once the design has been completed.

The Problems Become the Focus, Eclipsing the Positive Points

It's quite difficult, sometimes impossible, to be objective about your own living space because you are so involved in its original purchase, the up-keep, and the minutia of day-to-day 'challenges'. In addition it's all too easy to get caught up in the irritation factor of an issue, rendering you unable to take a step back when thinking about a solution.

The Importance of Structure is Overlooked in Favour of Plants

I often see a tendency among garden owners to think of the garden in terms of just the planting. I can see why this happens, especially when you look at a perennial border in full bloom, but that is only looking at one dimension of the garden.

A strong layout is needed to make the garden feel like a garden should.

Forgetting to Factor 'Time' into the Equation

By its very nature, a garden will grow and change. This must be taken into account when starting to plan it. The effects of time must be allowed for in a garden, more so than any other place. It is possible you do not have much experience or knowledge about this, which can make starting the garden a daunting exercise.

Completely Underestimating the Value of Soil

Soil is the soul and foundation of every garden, and its characteristics will dictate which plants will grow with success and what will fail. The important characteristics to find out about are how well it drains, whether it is sand, loam or clay soil, and whether it is Neutral, Acidic or Alkaline. These are naturally occurring characteristics you can do little about. You also need to evaluate whether your soil is healthy or not, which is something you *can* change. A very common mistake is the planting of heathers and rhododendrons in soils that do not let them thrive. Both plants need acidic (also known as ericaceous) soil and without it, they will slowly but surely die.

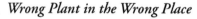 *Wrong Plant in the Wrong Place*

This is a major one. Plants in the wrong place do one of two things. They either die and you waste your money, or they become a nuisance by getting too big or invading the rest of the garden. A good example of this is the planting of mint, which – once established – grows everywhere with great vigour. The same goes for some members of the bamboo family, among others.

Summary

This chapter paints a picture of doom and gloom, but all is not lost! By using the Three Foundation Steps that make up The Garden Equation, you will have a very powerful tool at your disposal, and an effective methodology for acquiring the information you need to make your garden a delightful part of your lifestyle. Although it's very useful to know what you are up against, and why you find it difficult to move to the next stage with your garden, the following chapters will give you the means to overcome the feelings of helplessness and overwhelm. When you know what you want to do in your garden, what the physical conditions are that must be taken into consideration, and what the maintenance implications are, you will be amazed at how easy it becomes to see past the short-term obstacles identified in this chapter, and make decisions that turn your garden into a manageable and enjoyable part of your life.

 CASE STUDY OF A COMMON MISTAKE

Here is an example of the power of objectivity in action. I once went to see a lady who had a charming house in a very pretty North Yorkshire village. Her small garden was beautiful and a real credit to her, but she was desperate to find a way to reduce the impact of the new silage tower that had been put up in the field next to her, especially as it was the biggest thing in the immediate landscape and it dominated the patio, where she had a lovely old table and chairs. She told me she'd thought and thought about it but couldn't find a solution. Although this seems a little over the top, she told me she was ready to sell.

I could see her point (not to mention the eyesore in question), but I could also see a solution which had not occurred to the lady. This is where being in a position of objectivity was invaluable. As I had not been through the experience of objecting to the planning permission, watching the tower being built, and then having my eyes drawn inexorably to it every day, being as it was opposite the kitchen window, my thoughts and opinions were unencumbered with the irritation and vexation that were affecting the owner. As a result, I could look at the situation impassively and saw that there was a simple answer.

My solution was to move the patio to the end of the garden, which would still locate it close enough to the house to be practical, but would allow me to turn her focus away from the silage tower (now behind her), and towards the house. The lady of the house could no longer see the eye sore when eating outside, and a couple of well placed, well-chosen trees, planted along the bottom wall, gave her something much nicer to look at from the kitchen window. This enabled her to accept the situation and enjoy her garden.

Chapter 2

Know What You Want

Before getting going with the Three Foundation Steps, I want to make a suggestion that I hope you will adopt throughout the process described in this book. I think the underlying key to succeeding with your garden lies in changing the way you think about it. Think about your garden as though it is as much a part of your immediate living space as any of the rooms in your home, and make your decisions about it accordingly. What happens outside can have a big impact on your lifestyle, so you want to do everything you can to ensure that you get what you want. The phrase 'outdoor room' was first used by garden designer John Brookes, MBE, in his ground-breaking book *Room Outside*, published in 1969. The concept is not new. I do, however, think that this is a good moment to draw your attention to it, so you can hold the notion in the back of your mind as you work through the Three Foundation Steps.

Step One: The Experience of the Garden

Time spent working out what you really want to do or have in the garden is never wasted, but sadly this step is often neglected or rushed in the enthusiasm to get going. In fact, time spent on this step is one of the best investments you will ever make. You will save yourself a lot of wasted time, energy, and money in the long run. More than that, this step will give you the motivation to carry on with the garden until you have got it exactly right for you.

In order to work out what you want to do in your garden you should create a Foundation List of what is important to you. What would you most like to do and experience in your garden? Consider this in combination with the practical things that make the space workable. The items on the Foundation List start the design process and will become the backbone of the finished garden. If your garden was a loaf of risen bread, Step One is the equivalent of putting the yeast into the mix.

The Foundation List doesn't need to be long or complicated, but whatever is on it needs to be as *truthful* and *detailed* as possible. Aim to have things on there that will enhance your lifestyle and create a delightful and enjoyable experience outside. In this chapter, I will explain more fully what I mean and give examples, so you have an idea what you are aiming for. The goal by the end of this chapter is to have created your own personal Foundation List.

The Practicals

When creating your Foundation List, consider the practical issues involved in your garden. You need to work out what needs to be included, in order to make your life easy and manageable. One of the major principles of all design disciplines is that 'Form follows function'. It would have been very easy to just discuss the enjoyable elements of garden design, but if the practical elements are not in place it doesn't matter how delightful the rest of the garden is, there will always be an underlying niggle of irritation, however well-buried, when it comes to the logistics of day-to-day living. Listed below are the ones I see the most often, which years of experience has shown me are useful to think about now.

 Rubbish

Getting rid of rubbish and materials for recycling are the first thing to consider, on the simple basis that all households produce rubbish of some kind. The ideal you are aiming for is that the bins are very easy to access from the house, hidden from view, and straightforward to take out on bin day, even when full and heavy. As this ideal can only be achieved in a fraction of gardens, the consideration to concentrate on is finding somewhere to keep the bins that's easy to get to from your house. The way I assess the best place for them is to apply the Rainy Day test.

The Rainy Day Test

*How wet will you get putting rubbish out when it's pouring with rain?
If it's acceptable to you and the bins do not get in the way of other activities, then you have found your spot.*

Washing Line

Where will you hang the laundry? The garden design world is divided between the washing line and the whirligig, and both have pros and cons. Sometimes the amount of space you have will be the dictating factor, but if you have a choice, the ideal to aim for with either method is a spot in the sun, not underneath a tree, that is easy to get to without it getting too muddy underfoot when it's wet. Consider the visual invasion, particularly of a washing line, on the overall garden. I find it quite extraordinary how much impact a single line can have when it's strung across an open space. Possible compromise solutions are to use a retractable washing line or a whirligig and put them away when not in use.

Access Paths

A beautiful winding path can be a delight, but not if you want to get from your garage to your house on a dark night, or while laden with the week's shopping. Decide where you need to get to, and from - for practical purposes only at this point. For example, you will need to get from the house to the garage, shed, bin area, compost bins, green house, washing line etc. These paths are not the focus of the design but you will become irritated if you can't access these areas directly, and they need to be mentioned in the brief at the beginning. The most important path to remember is the one to the front door. It needs to be practical, stylish, and to the point!

Shed

Sheds are the ultimate in multifunctional storage spaces and as such are very useful. I think most gardens would benefit from having some sort of storage for outside things. Some gardens I've seen have the tiniest little sheds, while others are overwhelmed and dominated by one. I recently designed a garden for a lady who had just moved into a newly-built home, the design of which had been done with great care, with every detail beautifully executed, including a bespoke shed to fit the awkwardly shaped garden. All well and good, except that the shed took up one third of the total available outside space. It looked like a continuation of the accommodation. I could see that the shed had been designed with the proposed usage in mind, but no thought had been given to its proportion, the impact it had on the rest of the garden, and how the space surrounding it would be used. The solution was to take the shed down and use the space for what the client really wanted. Sheds are very useful but they need to be in proportion.

Garden and Kitchen Waste

It is very prudent to plan how you are going to get rid of the inevitable waste. There are three viable options. You can have one, or two, compost bins. They are environmentally friendly and you expend little energy in depositing the garden waste in them. They do, however, need to be used correctly to avoid it all drying out or turning into a smelly sludge, and you need to have space for them.

You can bag it up in sturdy black plastic bags and tuck them away out of sight until the following year. This is a less precise approach to compost but it usually produces something useful if you are prepared to wait long enough. Again, you need to have somewhere to leave the bags, and they can be heavy to move about.

The final choice is only viable if you have a council that provides you with a garden waste bin. A lot of people contribute to the council-run composting schemes, especially when you can buy the compost back at a small cost. My local council assured me that the compost that is available to buy back is clean, which I really hope is true because I know I've contributed some real plant nasties over the years.

What Would You Like to Experience in the Garden?
Consider what sort of experience you want your garden to give you. A common misconception is that many people view their gardens only as places in which they can do or have things. When the usage of a garden is restricted like this, you are only enjoying half the available experience. It's a bit like watching television with no sound.

A garden will evoke an emotion in you whatever happens, because outside spaces connect with your sub-conscious whether you like it or not. Often a garden can feel right or 'like a garden should' by instinct, or because the garden designer has done a good job. I think it would be much more satisfying if you decide for yourself how you'd like the garden to feel.

A lady I once met said, 'Gardens talk to the heart as well as to the eyes', and her words have stayed with me. Although I have no formal qualification in the way humans think, I do know from experience that we all like beauty and order to be part of our lives in some form, and the garden is a wonderful place to realise both these elements. When a place is in order you can feel safe, tranquil, comfortable, at ease, peaceful, and relaxed. When the same place is beautiful as well, you can feel joyful, delighted and content. If the combination between order and beauty is the right one for you, you can also feel invigorated, recharged and re-energised by spending time outside.

*My garden is my most
beautiful masterpiece*

CLAUDE MONET

It can be difficult to transform a design made on an emotional level into a reality, and I failed to do so for ages. When I had been in horticultural college for only 6 weeks and my lack of experience was still profound, my grandmother asked a neighbour of hers to have a chat with me, 'Because I think he's a landscape architect and he might be able to help you'. I went along and there followed an afternoon on the subject of designing landscapes for the subconscious, which blew my mind. It was too much, too soon for me, and a lot of it was wasted on me at the time. Now, eighteen years later, I understand exactly what my gran's neighbour meant.

My grandmother's neighbour was Sir Geoffrey Jellicoe, a man of enormous experience, wisdom and skill in creating people-friendly landscapes. The day I spent with him I was in total ignorance of the eminence in which he was internationally held. I only later found out that he was a founding member of the Landscape Institute, its president for ten years, trustee of the Tate Gallery, London, designer of many huge and important public schemes all around the world - including the Kennedy Memorial Garden in Runnymeade, the water gardens in Hemel Hempstead and the Moody Gardens in Galveston, Texas, to name but three. He'd also written sixteen books in his time.

To illustrate what Geoffrey Jellicoe talked to me about, I will use a simple garden bench as an example.

To him it was much more important to make a place feel right to the people who used the space. Many people see the garden as a place to relax in, and an example of a physical item representing this could be to have a bench in the evening sun, on which to enjoy a glass of wine. While it's not difficult in the slightest to physically sit on a bench, the action and experience will only be classed as enjoyable if you can relax and wind down. In order for you to do this, the atmosphere in this part of the garden must be tranquil, calming, and peaceful. Hence, in this example, tranquillity is something that needs identifying as a requirement for the design.

Although this is a complex area, I've found a good way to identify the important underlying emotions for the garden is to look behind the activity you want to do, or the item you want to have, and work out what atmosphere is required to make that experience the best it can possibly be, as I showed you with the example of the bench.

This is not an aspect of The Garden Equation to get stuck on, and you will be doing well if you can come up with two examples. The emotional side of things does tend to work out by working through the Three Foundation Steps, but it is always worth being aware that this is a consideration.

The 'Doing' Things

This is probably the part that is easiest to dream about and to visualize in situ, although the size and orientation of the garden will dictate how much of your Requirement List can be accommodated

Relaxing

This is the main thing people use their gardens for and it's one of those ambiguous words that means many things to many people, so have a think about what this means to you. I've had the following definitions in client briefs over the years:

- Looking at a nice view, which could be beyond your garden boundaries or at a beautiful border in full flower
- Having their own space in privacy
- Having a cup of tea, coffee, or glass of wine
- Watching the sun go down
- Eating outside
- Gardening
- Having friends round
- Chatting
- Cooking
- Watching wildlife
- Mowing the lawn
- Playing games, such as boules
- Reading

- Praying or meditating
- Socialising
- Enjoying the sight and sound of water
- Sowing seeds, planting plants
- Being in the green house
- Looking at a wildflower meadow
- Feeding the birds/squirrels/hedgehogs
- Having somewhere for the dog to run about in
- Keeping chickens/pets

Experience has given me some perspective on certain points from the list above, which may be useful for you:

 Eating Outside

Eating outside, even in the unpredictable weather of the British Isles, is still the number one activity that people want to do. Personally, I think that having a table and chairs permanently outside and always available encourages more usage, so if possible put this in your brief. Other considerations with eating outside is the location of the table and chairs, which should be within reasonable access of the kitchen, unless there is an overwhelming reason to place them somewhere else.

Make sure the patio for the table and chairs is big enough for sensible usage. It is surprising how much space is required for a table and chairs, so

I always start with the size of the table and then design the patio to fit round it. Once the size and the shape of the table has been decided, the thing to take into account is the space needed to let the chairs be used comfortably. Try measuring how much space it takes to pull a chair out, sit down, and then push it out from the table to stand up. You also want to allow for space to move round the table so all in all it usually requires $4m^2$ for an average 1.8 x 1.00m rectangular table.

Cooking Outside

If you love eating outside, then you might consider having a built in BBQ, a permanent work surface, or somewhere that's easy on the back to place your moveable BBQ - assuming it has no stand. Some people even have running water plumbed into their outdoor kitchen. Pizza or bread ovens are gaining in popularity and they need to be located in the right place, depending on what they are made of and the direction of the wind. They also need to conform to the Clean Air Act 1993 (contrary to popular opinion).

Entertaining

When thinking about entertaining, you need to think about the type of get-togethers you mostly prefer. If you go for gatherings where the guests stand up, you have more flexibility as to where it all happens. If your entertaining centres round sit down meals, then the points already discussed will dictate how much space is required. If you usually have drinks parties, then the location where these take place can be further from the kitchen - do not forget to consider access.

Gardening

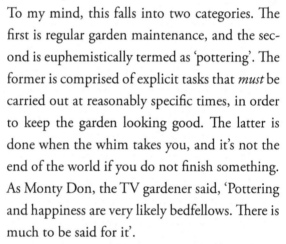

To my mind, this falls into two categories. The first is regular garden maintenance, and the second is euphemistically termed as 'pottering'. The former is comprised of explicit tasks that *must* be carried out at reasonably specific times, in order to keep the garden looking good. The latter is done when the whim takes you, and it's not the end of the world if you do not finish something. As Monty Don, the TV gardener said, 'Pottering and happiness are very likely bedfellows. There is much to be said for it'.

Believe it or not, the activity (or inactivity) of 'pottering' needs to be planned for, but I'll talk about this in more detail when discussing the Third Foundation Step: Maintenance Considerations.

Time of Year

Identify the time of year you are most likely to be at home, as this will dictate the kind of garden you will have. I've just spoken to a man whose family go abroad from May to September, but are in the UK in the late autumn, winter, and early spring months. He wants his garden to look more interesting during the time he is in the UK, so he has a garden that has autumn colours, winter interest, and early spring bulbs in it. Another client is an avid horse racing fan, so she requires her garden to be low maintenance in the summer months because she is away for many weekends and often has other commitments during the week. Neither of these gardens would be the source of joy I know they are if the question of what time of year the client wanted to spend most time in their garden hadn't been asked.

Think About What You Can See of the Garden from the House

The UK has many grey, cold, and wet days, which keep people inside. Instead of writing the garden off during the inhospitable times of year, think about whether you can see anything of interest from the windows of the most frequently used rooms. I can see the only tree in my garden from my bedroom window perfectly, as my line of site goes straight into the canopy. It is an old, gnarled, damson tree, and it is the most wonderful sight to see it in full bloom every April. The flowers come out before the leaves appear, so when it is in full swing the tree is a cloud of delicate blooms. Another tip is to plant spring bulbs close to the house, so their bright colours can be seen and enjoyed fully from inside. The same goes for any feature or specimen plant. Ask yourself if they are visible from the house, as well as being visible while in the garden; this way you get double value for your money.

Wildlife

Wildlife is remarkably unfussy. If you want to attract wildlife into the garden, it is not necessary to plant exclusively native plants - although having some is beneficial. A great example is something I've been using in clients' gardens for the past five years, and that is to sow an annual meadow. You can now buy carefully thought-out mixes of annual flowers that have been put together to create a carpet of jewelled colours in succession over the summer months and into autumn. These meadows are alive with insects, particularly bees, and only approximately one third of the varieties used are native.

Water in the garden is a fantastic resource for wildlife and a source of great entertainment to the watcher. You must, however, decide from the onset whether the pond is to be for ornamental fish or wildlife, because you cannot have both in the same pond.

Birds will always be attracted to gardens where there is food, water, and enough shelter for them to perch and nest, such as hedges, shrubs, and trees.

Safety

Think about the people who will be using the garden, in addition to you. If you have children, or know there will be children visiting regularly, you may want to think, for example, about how to make the pond safe, so you can relax without worrying about what the children are up to. The same might apply to other features, such as trees or a rockery. You could also think about how people with walking difficulties might negotiate your garden and perhaps put a hand rail on steps. Reduce any trip hazards or install lighting at specific points.

Privacy

This is an important aspect to think about right from the start, because no garden is enjoyable if it is overlooked, or you feel exposed. A lack of privacy is one of the biggest issues that stop people from relaxing. This is the main reason that few people sit out in their front gardens, because they are not, by their very nature, private places.

Privacy, or lack of it, comes in varying degrees. At its most public, your garden will be open to anyone being able to see in, as happens when you have no fence or hedge between you and a public street or place. At its least public, your garden will be completely private, with no one able to see into it at all. Most people, however, and especially those who live in urban situations, have gardens where a part of it is private and other areas are less so. In those situations, you will have to take a view as to whether you can live with it comfortably or whether you need to take further steps to create privacy.

*We can complain because rose
bushes have thorns, or rejoice
because thorn bushes have roses.*

ABRAHAM LINCOLN

What You Do not Want

Sometimes it's easier to write down what you do not want. You might have a strong view about a particular colour or plant and it's useful to know about it in advance. I've had a number of clients say that they do not like yellow and want nothing whatsoever of that colour in their garden. I even had it that some lilies that I planted, which were labelled as pink Stargazers, came up yellow and the client asked me to remove them immediately, when the first bud appeared. She was quite annoyed - not at growing the wrong lilies but at having to look at something yellow.

A Few Words of Wisdom Born from Experience...

It's well worth writing your thoughts down because this is the first step in the process of getting your ideas out of your head and into reality. It can also help in clarifying your thoughts, which is useful when communicating them to someone else. One of the main traps to avoid is to assume that your approach is the common one that everyone takes. It isn't, because every garden and every owner will have a different Foundation List, in combination with different garden conditions, even if comparing two gardens that are identical in size and right next door to each other. In eighteen years I have come across a wide variety of differing ideas about what people want to do and have in their gardens, and every single one of them thought that their approach was the 'norm'.

The more detail you can go into, the better. I had one client who started off so vaguely that all she wanted was 'something nice'. What on earth does that mean? For example, I think it would be nice to have a natural swimming pool in my garden, but I know many people would shudder at the thought - this particular client most certainly didn't want one, yet to me, that is 'something nice'.

There is no right or wrong answer about what to do or have in your garden, and I've not yet come across anything that I thought was too strange or unattainable to at least think about. An example of some of the more unusual things I've been asked for include a garden for a miniature steam train with a 6" gauge track (which they got), a lighthouse (which they did not get), a labyrinth (which is ongoing), a 50ft radio mast (which was difficult to blend in!), an adult tree house (which is still being built), and a jungle (which they did not get). It is well worth while to take a little time over this and to sleep on it, as things will occur to you, particularly in different weather conditions and at different times of the day.

If someone else is involved in making decisions about the garden, include them in the discussion from the start. If you talk about having a pond but do not discuss where it is to be positioned, it's quite possible that the other person sees it in a different place to you, for different - and perhaps just as valid- reasons and this can lead to heated debates that could have been avoided.

 CASE STUDIES

Although I've written quite a bit about all the different things to consider when drawing up the Foundation List, your initial list might be quite short. Here are several first drafts of Foundation Lists from previous clients. This first list may seem insignificant but do not underestimate it or write it off because it will probably show you the things that are most important to you.

Client 1

- Space to play with grandchildren - particularly with a sandpit
- Somewhere that feels relaxing
- A lawn
- Gentle curves
- Somewhere to read that is out of the sun (having had several melanomas)

Client 2

- A tranquil pond to attract wildlife
- A 'gin and tonic' bench in the evening sun, to wind down on at the end of the day
- One or two small fruit trees (a 'crumble' tree, was the exact phrase used)
- Eating outside
- Space for herbs near the kitchen door

Client 3

- A patio that would accommodate eating outside and entertaining friends
- A pizza oven and/or a BBQ
- A wall-mounted water feature on the patio
- A chicken run

Client 4

- A swing seat - the client had one as a child and always wanted one as an adult
- A pond with goldfish
- A patio in the sun, as the client was from Spain and she loved to sunbathe
- A bench at the top of the garden to enjoy the view
- An organic vegetable garden

Client 5

- An evening patio to make the most of the setting sun, as this aspect had the nicest view and the client was only at home in the evenings
- Low maintenance
- Scented plants, particularly those in the area of the patio
- A decent, flat lawn that was easy to mow
- Screening from the road as the garden owner felt exposed when out in the garden

All these Foundation Lists, when applied to the specific gardens of their owners, would begin to give a shape to how the design of the garden would be. For example, several of the clients who's Foundation Lists are given above wanted patios or benches from which to enjoy the evening sun. Since there is absolutely no choice where that patio or bench has to go to achieve this, as the sun comes up in the east and goes down in the west, one element of the design is already in place.

Summary

Have a go at writing the first draft of your Foundation List now, by doing the following:

1. List all the practical things you must have to make the garden functional

2. List one or two emotional aspects, if you can, but do not spend too much time worrying about this if nothing comes to mind

3. List all the things you would love to do in the garden

4. List all the things you would love to have in the garden

5. Sleep on it

6. Discuss it with an objective person AND anyone else who lives in the house with you.

Chapter 3

Identifying the Growing Conditions in Your Garden and Why They Are Important

The second Foundation Step is identifying the physical growing conditions that are naturally present in your garden. The point of this step is to find out what you have already got in the garden, then work on maximizing the existing opportunities, rather than trying to change them. By doing so you are giving yourself the best opportunity to have an enjoyable, beautiful, and thriving garden.

Soil

To me, the soil is the soul of the garden. I sincerely hope to convince you of this approach. Soil characteristics will have an effect on every single plant you put in the ground. In turn, this will affect the appearance of the garden as a whole, and will impact on the amount, frequency, and intensity of work you have to expend in maintenance.

To be blunt, the soil will either cost you or help you. It doesn't care which. Nature will always win, because it plays the long game and knows how to wait.

Soil Types and How to Identify Them

There are four main types of soil: Clay, Sand, Silt, and Loam. Each is made up from a combination of the same materials: clay, sand, and silt. Clay particles are the smallest, sand particles are the largest, and silt particles are in between. It is the ratio of one ingredient to another that dictates the positive and negative aspects of your soil. In addition, you can have a peat soil, which is made up of mostly organic matter (making it acidic), and a chalky soil, which is mostly comprised of calcium carbonate (and therefore very alkaline) - more about this aspect later.

Soil types can vary within a very small area, so I recommend that you check your soil in several places in the garden.

How to Test Your Soil Type

To find out what sort of soil you have got, take a small amount between your finger and thumb and roll it into a ball.

If it forms a tacky, cohesive ball, you have a **clay soil**.

If there is no cohesive lump of soil and it feels very gritty, you have a **sandy soil**.

Silty soils feel 'soapy' when rolled between the finger and the thumb. Although silty soils do form a ball, it is much looser than a clay ball and it will feel smooth rather than sticky.

You have **loamy soil** if you can squeeze some of your soil in your hand and it will hold its shape, but fall apart if given a light prod. This is regarded as the perfect soil and you are *very* lucky if you have it without having to put in a lot of hard work.

Clay Soils

Clay soils, also known as heavy soils, are those that are high in clay particles, with some silt and very little sand. Another way you will know you have a soil with clay in it is that clay soils tend to take a lot of effort to work (hence the term *heavy* is applied). On days when weather conditions make it too wet for cultivation, you can even dig a decent hole using a garden fork (not recommended) as clay soil is so sticky and claggy.

 What To Take Into Account With Clay Soil

Clay soil is heavy to work with, takes a long time to cultivate, and will compact very easily, due to the smallness of the particle size, especially in the wet months. In the summer, clay soils can dry out leaving you with rock hard clods, or cracks in the soil, which are very difficult to work with and incredibly difficult to rehydrate. Clay soils warm up slowly and drain slowly, which means the growing season is shorter than with other soils.

 WHAT IS COMPACTION?

Compaction occurs when the tiny gaps between soil particles have been squashed together. This prevents oxygen from getting into the soil, resulting in a rank smelling, unworkable lump.

Compaction also prevents water from draining away properly, which leads to water-logged, squelchy soil.

No plant will thrive, and most will die, in compacted or water-logged soil.

The Good News About Clay Soils

Clay is the most naturally occurring fertile soil, of all the different soil types, over the longest period. It holds water well, so drought conditions have much less of an impact on the plants within it. If it is respected and managed sensibly it is the soil that will serve you the longest, and the one that plants will do well in. Provided the soil is not compacted, winter conditions will also carry on the breaking-down process.

Although clay does require maintenance, once you have done what you were going to do by way of major cultivation and improvement, it can generally be left, year on year, with just a little work annually.

Final Thoughts on Clay Soils

Some plants, such as lavenders, have come from places where they have had to adapt to free draining soils. These are the types of plant to avoid when buying plants for heavy soils. A general rule of thumb is that any plant that has silver foliage, hairy leaves, or is from the Mediterranean area, is not suitable for planting in clay. However, any plant that can cope with some moisture retention in the soil will thrive and look wonderful. As clay soils can compact very easily, it is probably not a good idea to plant annuals, or anything else that will require regular moving or replacing.

A well-worked clay soil that is not walked on is a hard-working soil that repays the effort that goes into it, with interest! For tips and plant suggestions for clay soils, go to:

www.yorkshiregardendesigner.co.uk/Toolbox

Sandy soils

Sandy soils are the opposite of clay soils. They have a big, open structure, with lots of sand and very little clay in them.

What To Take into Account With Sandy Soil

Sandy soils drain very quickly and therefore dry out fast, so it is possible that newly placed plants will suffer, or existing ones will wilt in hot and/ or windy conditions. This can result in the need for watering in the height of the summer. As a result of their exceptional drainage, sandy soils are usually low in naturally occurring nutrients, which get washed away easily. This is also true of any nutrients applied by you, so regular mainte-nance will be required to sustain the fertility of the soil and the health of the plants.

The Good News About Sandy Soils

Sandy soils are easy to dig and cultivate, so you are less likely to damage your back and you can achieve results more quickly. An advantage of their excellent drainage qualities means the roots of your plants will almost never rot off in wet conditions, or suffer from any of the issues that water-logged soils have. Due to the large particle size, the cohesion caused by capillary action between each particle is considerably less than that found in a clay soil. The big advantage of this is that the gaps are bigger, and therefore sandy soils are well aerated and well drained, resulting in the least amount of compaction out of all the soil types. They also warm up quickly so you will get quicker plant establishment and growth in the spring.

Final Thoughts on Sandy Soil

If you have sandy soil, the best plants to use are those that like free-draining conditions, and can possibly withstand some degree of drought. You will also need to think about how to maintain this kind of soil. You can find tips and plant suggestions on this at:

www.yorkshiregardendesigner.co.uk/Toolbox

Silty Soils

Silt particles are bigger than clay but smaller than sand.

Things To Take into Account With Silty Soil

Due to the presence of sand within a silty soil, the structure will still break down readily, but because of the clay and silt, it will become compacted easily. It is also fine, meaning it can be blown away when the soil is bare, dry, and the wind is strong enough, which it often is in this country.

The Good News About Silty Soil

Compared to a sandy soil, silty soils are more fertile and hold more water. In comparison to a clay soil, they are well drained. Less effort is required to cultivate these soils and they do not require quite so much ongoing maintenance.

Loamy Soils

There is nothing negative to take into account with a loamy soil.

The Good Bits About Loamy Soil

It is fertile, and well-drained, but retains enough moisture for excellent plant growth. It has a good structure, meaning it does not compact easily. It warms up quickly in spring, which means it offers a long growing season. It is easily worked and does not dry out in the summer.

If you have this soil, you have been blessed!

Soil pH and How to Test For It

The abbreviation 'pH' stands for 'possible Hydrogen' (should you be curious!).

All soils have a pH number, which indicates how acidic or alkaline it is. A pH of 7 is Neutral, less than 7 is Acidic, and above 7 is Alkaline.

pH 3 - 5, your soil is very acidic and will most likely be poor in nutrients. This is because nutrients are more soluble at these pH values, and will have probably been washed away.

pH 5.1 - 6, your soil is acidic, which is ideal for all ericaceous plants, such as rhododendrons, heathers, and camellias.

pH 6.1 - 7, your soil is moderately acidic to neutral. A pH of 6.5 is the best general-purpose value for earthworms and bacterial to function at, and provides the highest degree of solubility for plant nutrients.

pH 7.1 – 8, your soil is alkaline, and you cannot plant acid-loving plants in it. The scale stops at 8.

Why You Need to Know Your Soil pH

You need to know the pH of your soil because there are some plants that can only grow in soils of a certain pH value. Some are quite tolerant, but others are not. One of the most well-known and loved plants that people commonly make this mistake with is the rhododendron. For this plant to flourish, it must be planted in acidic soil. When it's not, it will slowly die, because it is unable to access all the nutrients it needs from the soil. The classic indicator that this is happening is when the leaves go yellow in between the veins, in a process called chlorosis (chlorosis is also caused by other conditions, but it is the most obvious symptom of the placement of acid-loving plants in neutral to alkaline soil).

How to Test the pH Value of Your Soil

Soil pH is easily tested for by using an inexpensive, quick, simple-to-use kit that is available at most garden centres. The instructions are very straightforward. You do not have to have any scientific training to use them, but if you would like to see a short video about using a pH kit, go to: www.yorkshiregardendesigner.co.uk/Toolbox

Shade and Sun

The areas in your garden with the most sun will be the most productive, especially in the summer when the sun is warm, and present for longer periods. These are the ideal places to put favourite plants, or those you are eager to see do well.

 What to Do

Observe your garden and make a note of which areas get the sun and for how long (approximately). The same goes for the shady areas, though for these you also need to know how much sun they do or do not get. The different categories of shade are: **dappled shade**, which means an area that gets a mix of sun and shade for most of the day; **partial/light shade**, which means an area that gets full sun, for less than half the day; and **dense shade**, which means an area that gets no sun, or only a little at the height of the summer.

What Affects the Amount of Sun You Get in Your Garden?

Orientation

The direction, or aspect that your garden faces, impacts throughout. When looking at this in relation to your garden, it is the direction that the main part of the garden faces *towards* that is the important factor, because the direction the sun shines *from* will dictate how much light and shade you do or do not get. A south-facing garden is considered the warmest, and can get continuous sun from midday onwards, depending on the givens for each site. West- and south-west-facing gardens will get the evening sun, while east-facing ones will get the morning sun. My own garden is east-facing, so it is beautifully sunny in the morning but quite shaded in the evening. North-facing gardens usually require more thought, but with the right plants you can still have a lovely garden - even though they get the least amount of sun and warmth, and are usually damper.

Hedges, fences, walls, and buildings will also cast shade into your garden.

How to Find Out the Direction Your Garden Faces

There are several methods that are easy to hand. Most smart phones have a compass on them. You can put your postcode into Google Earth and have an aerial look at your garden. I like doing this, as you see your garden from a completely different perspective, and North is always marked pointing to the top of the screen. Alternatively you could use a handheld compass.

If these options do not appeal, or are unavailable to you, you can simply note where the sun rises in the morning, and where the sun falls the most during the day. It doesn't really matter whether you know the orientation, as long as you know where the sun falls during the day, especially during the summer.

Why You Need to Know This

Not all plants can cope with full sun, others need full sun, and many can only deal with partial or dappled shade, not dense shade. If a plant needs more light than it is getting it will 'look' for it by growing upwards, becoming long and leggy in the process. This results in a straggly, weak plant that won't look very nice. The foliage of plants put in full sun, when they really need the respite of a bit of shade, will scorch and turn brown or become bleached white, which again doesn't look very nice and results in a weak plant. Variegated plants will also lose their variegation if they receive too much sun.

Rainfall

High ground, hills, and mountain ranges can influence the amount of rain fall you get, either excessively or not and it also depends which side of the country you live in. If you look at the average annual rainfall for the whole of the UK, as shown on a map (see http://bit.ly/UKRainfall), you will see that the west side of the country gets far more rain than the east. Blackpool, on the west coast, got an annual average of 871.3mm of rain between 1971 and 2000. Cleethorpes, on the east coast, only got 564.4mm over the same period. That's a big difference, which will significantly influence what plants will grow best for you.

 ### Why You Need to Know This

Plants need water to survive! Watering can be time-consuming, and expensive if you are on a water meter. In areas of low rainfall, it is a good idea to mulch your borders and use plants that are drought-tolerant. It could also be worth investing in an irrigation system, such as those that use porous pipes, especially if you are away from home for periods longer than a week to 10 days.

If you know what the average annual rainfall is in your area, then look for plants that can cope with the conditions produced by that amount of rain, in conjunction with your soil type. So that you know roughly what you are dealing with, areas with more than an average of 800mm of rain a year are considered to get *high* amounts of rain, while those with an annual average of 600mm or less are in the *low* category (these figures apply to the UK and Ireland only). Just to put that all in perspective, St Osyth, Essex, gets an average annual rainfall of 507mm, and Dalness, Glen Etive, in the Highlands, gets a staggering average of 3300mm per year (Met. Office).

How to Find Out the Average Annual Rainfall in Your Area

The Met Office is a mine of information about the weather (http://www.metoffice.gov.uk). You can also find relevant information supplied by various other bodies, which seems to vary from region to region. I have found my local council website to be useful, as are the websites of the local newspapers and BBC Weather.

Topography and Wind

Wind is one of the most destructive elements to consider, because it dries out the soil, speeds up plant transpiration (leading to wilting, and ultimately death), and causes considerable physical damage too.

General topography will also have an effect of the growth-rate in your garden, because the higher you are above sea level, the colder your garden usually is, and the shorter the growing season.

Your garden might also be in a frost pocket, or have a frost pocket within it, which is another useful thing to know about. Frost pockets occur at the bottom of slopes, or at the base of something like a wall, which stops the cold air and allows it to 'pool'. If you imagine that the cold air is like water, it will slide down (being heavier than warmer air) to the lowest point, and there it stays until the general temperature warms up enough to dispel it. The implication of gardening in a frost pocket is that the plants must be hardy enough to survive conditions that are just a little bit colder than the rest of your area. My chickens live (unfortunately for them) in a frost pocket, and the change of temperature as I shut them up on frosty nights is quite noticeable. It's remarkable considering the change in the level they are at, compared to the rest of the garden, is only about 20cm. Luckily the chickens are well accustomed to their home now, after 3 years of living there.

Having talked about the force the wind can exert, most gardens have some sheltered spots, which are to be prized and optimised. Wind breaks can be introduced, but these require a surprisingly large amount of space to be effective, so they are not often viable in the average sized garden. It is quicker and more straightforward to note the sheltered spots that already exist, and to use them well.

Why You Need to Know This

Both the topography and the wind-chill factor will lower the temperature of the air and soil in your garden significantly, so it is very helpful to be aware that yours is more exposed than most, or simply that it is often very windy. It will be one of the first things you need to consider in order to work out how hardy the plants you buy need to be. Gardens in windy areas benefit greatly from a little extra maintenance, such as mulching your borders to stop the soil drying out. In my experience it is well worth considering plants that have become specifically adapted to the conditions. A good rule of thumb is to pick plants with thin leaves, such as grasses, because they have adapted to minimise the amount of water they lose through their leaves, and to provide the least amount of physical resistance to the wind when it blows.

How to Find Out About the Wind and Wind-Chill Factors in Your Garden

This is best done through personal observation of your own place over the period of a year. Ideally, this is something you do on an ongoing basis.

To help you, here are some clues to look for in your garden:

If your garden is exposed to a strong prevailing wind, the shape of the trees will show you exactly where it comes from. I'm sure you have seen trees in very exposed places bowed over by the wind? You are looking at something similar but not as extreme.

The wind-chill factor can also affect the way plants grow.

In the garden of one of my clients, I put four Ceanothus shrubs at the 4 corners of the lawn as part of a balanced planting scheme. Over the past 3 years, one has taken over its corner and one has not grown much at all, making the structured effect look lopsided. The largest Ceanothus had the advantage of growing in a slightly warmed microclimate, being protected from the wind by the garage, while the smallest one took the full brunt of the wind. In the end, the difference in the size of the Ceanothus was so great we had to take them all out and replace them with something else.

TOP TIP

You could consider buying your own Home Weather Station and Rain Gauge. This way you will have the best and most accurate information about your specific garden.

Summary

Now you know how to find details about the following about your garden:

- How to identify soil types, and the differences between them
- How to test for soil pH and what different levels mean
- Sun and shade
- Rainfall
- Topography and wind

Have a look at the sketch I did for my garden on the next page and then have a go at finding the answers to these points yourself, and put them onto a sketch drawing of your garden.

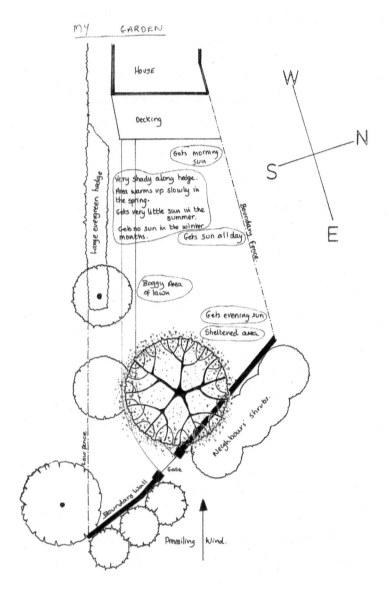

Chapter 4

Maintenance Considerations

The previous two Foundation Steps, discussed in the last two chapters, are an accepted part in the garden design process, and the majority of garden designs are (or should be) based on those two steps. They also occur reasonably early on in the process, as they form an integral part of the brief upon which the subsequent design is based. This third and final Foundation Step might seem out of place now, but once you have read the rest of this chapter, I think you will agree that it is essential to think about it now.

The third Foundation Step is to consider the maintenance implications of the proposed design or idea, *before anything is actually done in the garden*. I cannot see the point of creating and building a garden, which then goes on to become a nightmare to look after, because there is too much to do in the time its owner has allocated for its care. Logically, the time to think about this is *now* before any 'burdens' develop.

Maintenance is usually discussed as an after-thought once the garden has been created, and has traditionally had bad press. It is often regarded as one of those 'must-do' things in which there is little joy to be had. It is seen as the down-side of having an otherwise wonderful time in the garden. I find it really surprising that there seems to be little effort by the majority of designers (that I know), to tailor the care of the garden to fit the time that the owners have available to care for it.

The aim of this chapter is to show you the maintenance implications of your design choices, so that you stand a chance of making the right decisions to suit your lifestyle, whether you are starting with a new garden or reassessing your existing one The intention is to ensure that caring for your garden becomes part of the whole experience, rather than being seen as a necessary evil.

The ultimate goal is to convince you that the starting point of the design is the amount of time you can give to caring for your garden. The amount of care your garden requires must equal the time you can give to look after it, or else it will become a burden. All that starts with the concept design or Master Plan.

How Much Time Have You Got?

Work out how much time you realistically have to spend maintaining your garden. I call this your Core Maintenance Time – the minimum amount of time that you can give on a regular basis. The time you have for maintenance is NOT the same as the time you have for 'pottering' about the garden, which is different. Pottering describes a leisurely approach to doing enjoyable tasks in the garden, whereas maintenance involves specific tasks carried out and finished at specific times of year.

Clearly the size of your garden is a major factor in deciding how much time is needed, but I am working on the basis that if you class your garden as 'medium sized' and it is reasonably established (i.e. not brand new, or filled with weeds), you will need two to three hours a week, at the height of summer, for maintenance. If your garden is bigger than that, there should be no question about getting additional help with it.

Know What You Are Taking On

Things tend to become a burden when they turn out to be much bigger than expected and are unplanned for. Nobody likes to feel pressured and it's easy to allow feelings of overwhelm and resentment to set in. It's at this point that the enjoyment is dulled a little, and gradually the garden becomes less of a place for enjoyment and re-charging the batteries, and more of a task that 'should' be done.

The ideal situation to aim for is to be able to decide how the garden is going to be, being fully aware of the maintenance implication that those design choices will involve. So it is worth taking the time to work out a rough maintenance plan and what the implications are *before* the garden gets built or to get a realistic picture of what it takes to keep your existing garden in the condition you would like it to be in

Once you have completed Foundation Steps One and Two, this becomes achievable, because you know what you want to do in the garden in some detail, and what conditions you are going to have to deal with. Even if you know that the care of your garden is going to be in the hands of someone else, you still need to know roughly what skills to look for when hiring someone, and how much that will cost you, which is based on how many hours that person works for you.

I do not want you to think that I am advocating limiting yourself in anyway when it comes to deciding on what you want in the garden. The intention here is to give you an idea of what is involved in caring for the choices you make, with some alternatives to consider, so that you can realistically decide if the proposed design is the right one for you and your lifestyle.

Design Choices and Their Maintenance Implications

Of course there are many different potential garden styles. The style chosen will have a huge impact on the quantities and types of plants found in them, and therefore the amount of maintenance involved in looking after them. I cannot go through all the styles of gardens here, but I would like to make you aware that some styles are more labour-intensive than others.

Some gardens, such as *cottage gardens*, require a lot of maintenance - almost every day in the growing season - being a style with a lot of perennials and seasonally-dependent colour and interest. Others, such as *formal gardens* with a lot of clipped hedges and topiary, are labour intensive at certain times of the year, but require relatively little care in between.

Japanese/Chinese gardens are mostly based around trees and shrubs which are lower maintenance than perennials, and *gravel gardens* - if a weed suppressant membrane is used in conjunction with the gravel - require very little weeding.

A garden always gives back
more than it receives.

MARA BEAMISH

Perennial Borders (Herbaceous Borders)

The Contribution Perennials make to the Garden

In my view, there is nothing more arresting and beautiful than to see a perennial border in full flower. Perennials give you the opportunity to enjoy a wide variety of colour combinations, textures, scents, heights, and seasonal attributes, in a relatively small space. They also recover more quickly from damage than a shrub or a tree, and I think there is always a perennial to fit into your garden, whatever size you have available.

Advantages of Using Perennials to Lower Maintenance

Perennials grow quite quickly, so if your border has been planned properly you will buy enough plants to fill the bed, and prevent the weeds from gaining a foot hold, within two to three growing seasons - depending on how big the root system was when planting.

Should a plant die, it's very easy and quick to replace it, and it could be enjoyable too, because it's an opportunity to try a new plant.

Maintenance Implications

Despite these benefits, as a gardener I believe borders that are mostly filled with perennials take the most amount of continuous care. The most relentless element of this is keeping them free of other plants that have no business being there i.e. weeds.

Other ongoing maintenance jobs for perennials include staking, dead-heading, splitting, replanting, mulching, soil care, and replacement. Every year, there will be fatalities from the winter weather, so new plants will need to be decided upon, bought, and planted to complement and enhance the overall scheme.

In addition to the actual physical aspects of care, creating a beautiful border that is filled with colour and interesting over several months takes knowledge, care, effort, and dedication to achieve. One of the most difficult and time-consuming looks to achieve is that of the 'traditional' *cottage garden*. Do not be fooled! Those lovely plants that 'just happened to ramble' into one another didn't do so all by themselves, nor did they stake, weed, or dead-head themselves either.

Care of perennials takes time on a regular basis during the growing season, with 'little and often' being the best formula to follow.

Many of my clients love doing all this and they do so in the full knowledge of what it takes to achieve a stunning border. That, to me, is success.

Shrubs

The Contribution Shrubs Make to the Garden

Areas of shrub planting can look amazing if planted thoughtfully and in-keeping with the surroundings. Most shrubs are not as flamboyant as some perennials but what they lack in vibrancy, they more than make up for with texture, leaf colour, berries, seeds, mass, and size.

Reasons for Using Shrubs in Reducing Maintenance

Once shrubs have been planted and start to grow, their branches and leaves create shade, and their roots - being bigger and better established - will have the greatest access to water and nutrients. As a result of this, weeds take longer to grow under shrubs, and tend to be weaker and stragglier than those grown in sunlight. By their very nature, it takes fewer shrubs to naturally help keep weeds at bay, and therefore it requires less time to look after that particular area.

Maintenance Implications

Shrubs themselves need maintaining, usually by pruning, but this tends to be done on an annual basis, and considerably less time is spent on them than would be required for a border of perennials.

Disadvantages of Using Shrubs

Shrubs are slower growing, tend to only flower once, and take up a lot more space than perennials, so it is not possible to have as much diversity and change of texture, colour, and scent, in shrubbery as a perennial border would bring.

Trees

The Contribution Trees make to the Garden

Trees bring vertical interest, leaf colour, blossom, fruit, berries and interesting bark to a garden, as well as being very beneficial to wildlife. Most gardens will benefit from at least one tree.

Reasons for Using Trees in Reducing Maintenance

Trees perform in much the same way as shrubs when it comes to shading and starving out the weeds. In fact there are some trees, such as conifers, whose roots form such a dense mat that almost nothing can grow beneath them.

Maintenance Implications of Trees

Fallen Leaves - Deciduous trees will always lose their leaves in the autumn. These leaves often need picking up to prevent other issues developing later on in the year. This task can be as big as the tree itself, and will take place over a number of days or weeks, depending on weather conditions. To put this into context, one fully mature sycamore tree will fill four to five wheelie bins with leaves. It might be tempting to just leave the leaves on the ground, but depending on their location, they will become slippery and dangerous if walked on, they can stain unsealed sandstone paving, and perpetuate the lifecycle of various pests and diseases.

Picking up fallen leaves can be very tedious and is not usually an enjoyable task. However, the good news is that it only happens once, at a specific time of year, so it can be planned for, and it does not require any particular horticultural skills to get the job done.

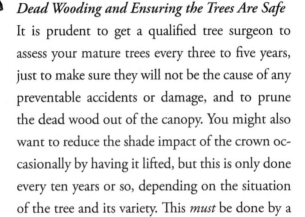 *Dead Wooding and Ensuring the Trees Are Safe*
It is prudent to get a qualified tree surgeon to assess your mature trees every three to five years, just to make sure they will not be the cause of any preventable accidents or damage, and to prune the dead wood out of the canopy. You might also want to reduce the shade impact of the crown occasionally by having it lifted, but this is only done every ten years or so, depending on the situation of the tree and its variety. This *must* be done by a professional. In my opinion, a tree should never be pruned into shape on an annual basis unless it's a yew or box. Instead, aim to plant the right tree for the space in the first place.

Although you yourself would/should never actually do the work of the tree surgeon, it will cost money to have someone who is qualified and professional to come and do it for you. Consequently there is a long-term cost implication of having trees in your garden.

Lawns
The word 'Lawn' means many things to many people, ranging from the very traditional stripe in a pristine

monoculture of green, to a varied, wild meadow. Both have their place and can be very beautiful, but one is much more labour- and time-intensive than the other.

Mowing is a bit like weeding in the perennial border. If you want a traditional pristine-looking lawn, it must be done regularly and consistently, every single week during the growing season. They also need to be aerated, fed, and treated for any diseases or non-grass plants such as moss. Mid-autumn is a good time to over-seed the bald patches, although this can be done in the spring too.

Wild flower meadows, or those with long grass, are much less labour intensive, and are therefore far easier to look after.

Ponds

Ponds also require maintenance, and it is a much-made mistake to think that they do not. The degree of maintenance is dictated by whether the pond is for wildlife, 'casual' fish, or 'serious' fish.

Wildlife ponds are the easiest to keep, as it is the intention that the proportion of plants in the pond use enough nutrients to prevent the development of 'green water' and algal blooms.

'Casual' fish ponds just have a few goldfish who are usually left to fend for themselves. They do not require feeding and there will be enough plants in the pond to absorb the extra nutrients provided by the fish droppings.

'Serious' fish ponds are another matter. They require regular cleaning and permanent filtering and aeration to prevent the build-up of excessive nutrients in the water, both from an aesthetic point of view, and for the well-being of the fish. The degree to which this is needed depends on the size of the pond and the numbers of the fish.

Action Plan

This should be done whether you are looking at a plan on paper or at your existing garden. Divide the garden into the main areas and then make a list of the maintenance actions required to keep that part looking like you want it to look. If there is something you do not know how to look after correctly, or you are a little unsure, look it up on the internet and make use of the incredible resource that is the World Wide Web. The Royal Horticultural Society (RHS) has a lot of information available about plants and gardening. This is an excellent site, but my personal favourite for information about maintenance is Shoot Gardening www.shootgardening.co.uk.

Once you have got the main maintenance activities down on paper, decide whether you like doing them all. If not, consider whether or not there is someone else who can do it for you?

Next, try and put a time scale on how long it takes you (or might take you) to complete the main activities in each area. It is not realistic for me to put down here how long things should or should not take to do, as there is no right or wrong answer; it varies from person to person and garden to garden.

This is a good time to point out that the right tools speed every action up, as does having a practical place to dispose of garden waste that is quick and easy to get to. Knowing what to do also helps get a job done quicker.

Finally, decide if the time you think is required to look after the garden fits in with the other calls on your lifestyle. If it does, that is good and you are on the right track for either carrying on with your existing garden, or going ahead with the new garden you are in the process of planning. If the garden looks like it could take up too much of your time, Chapter 6 is for you. If the garden has already become a burden, skip to Chapter 7 and where to get ideas and inspiration from is covered in Chapter 5.

If you are less than happy with the results of this particular process, do not despair, you are still only considering this on paper, not in reality. If you are thinking through the realities of your existing garden and you are not happy with your conclusions, now is the time to decide to make some changes.

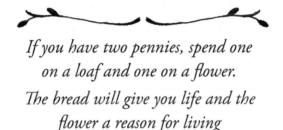

If you have two pennies, spend one
on a loaf and one on a flower.
The bread will give you life and the
flower a reason for living

CHINESE PROVERB

An Example of Maintenance Choices and Their Implications

Here is an example of the maintenance choices and their implications I asked a recent client to consider before their Master Plan had been finalized.

Lawn: Mowing

 Decide on the Type of Cut/Look You Like

If you want a very fine cut, then you will need a *cylinder mower* that will produce a good, striped finish, at very low levels. You will need to cut the lawn at least once a week during the growing season, which is approximately March to October, and twice a week during the summer.

If you are less particular about the look of the lawn and just want to keep it tidy, then a *rotary* or *hover mower* will do the job well. They cut less finely and cannot go down as low as a cylinder mower, but they can deal with uneven surfaces and longer grass. For this method, cut the lawn every seven to ten days. You can also raise the height of the mower, which will cut down on the amount of grass you take off, and therefore limit the amount you have to empty.

Do You Want to Collect the Grass Cuttings or Spread Them As You Go?

The three mowers discussed above all utilise collecting boxes, which you will have to empty. If you do not want to do this, then a *mulching mower* will chop up the grass cuttings very finely, and spread them out over the turf as you go. They will settle down at the base of the grass and the nutrients will gradually return to the soil. The only downside of a mulching mower is that if you use it on long grass you will have to rake the arisings up and dispose of them by hand, as leaving such large quantities on the surface of the turf will damage it.

Edging the Lawn

One of the best ways to prevent your garden becoming a mess is to keep the lawn well-edged. You must factor edging into your timings. This will be straightforward, as the shape of the lawn is already defined by the edge and path. Ensuring you have the best edging tool your budget will permit will also save you a great deal of time.

Time to Allow

It will probably take you an hour a week to look after the lawn.

An Alternative

An alternative to cutting the lawn is to let the grass grow long and let nature take its course.

One-Off Jobs

The lawn also requires weeding, feeding, scarifying, aeration and possibly re-seeding (at least the bald patches). These jobs are one-offs and take place in the spring and autumn.

Perennial Planting Area

These are the actions you will need to take to keep the perennial planting areas looking beautiful. Decide whether you are prepared to do this, whether there might be too much for you to care for or if you'd like to look for an alternative for these areas.

Plant Replacement

This can vary but it is quite common to have to fill gaps created by winter casualties.

Weeding

This is the job that should be done every week. I have found that it really helps to get on top of the weeds as soon as they appear in the spring time. It is particularly important to get the weeds out before they set seed in the late summer/early autumn.

Mulching

You can apply a mulch, at a minimum thickness of 30mm, to prevent seed-bourne weeds becoming established. Mulching also prevents the loss of water, through evaporation, from the soil surface, which will cut down on the amount of watering you might otherwise decide to do.

Deadheading

This will ensure that the plants flower for as long as possible, and should be done on a regular basis to ensure a continuous flow of flowers.

Staking

As some of the taller perennials grow, they will require staking. The plant grows into a better shape if the staking is done earlier rather than later.

Pests and Diseases

Keep a sharp eye out for anything that shows the plant is under attack. The sooner this is addressed the easier it is to eradicate or slow down the problem. You need to decide where you stand in relation to chemical versus organic solutions. In my experience it is quicker and often easier to use chemicals, but they can be harsh and detrimental to the surrounding environment. Organic solutions are gentler, but can be slower to achieve results.

Watering

You need to decide whether you will water during dry periods or let the plants take their chances. Alternatively you could invest in an irrigation system. These vary from a porous hose attached to the outside tap, to a fully automated, pop up system.

One-Off jobs

Perennials need to be split in the spring when they get too big, cut down in the autumn, and the surrounding soil dug over and enriched with well-rotted organic matter. Any areas of compaction or water-logging also need to be addressed.

Time to Allow

If done regularly, you will need to allow one to two hours a week during the growing season. If your efforts are more sporadic, they will require a greater investment of time on each occasion.

An Alternative

Replace some or all of the perennials with shrubs.

Wildflower Meadow

Decide on whether you want to have an annual meadow or a perennial meadow - the difference is in the amount of work required in establishment and cost.

Annual Meadow

The initial cost is low to buy the seeds, and the rest of the effort required to establish an annual meadow is in the labour, as the seed bed must be prepared correctly and thoroughly. This must be done every year.

Preparation of the seed bed could take half a day to do, but once the seeds have been sown, you do nothing more until the autumn and, even then, only if you do not like looking at the dead meadow.

You have to decide whether to apply a weed killer in the spring to get rid of last year's seeds, now growing, or if you will just rotavate the old vegetation back into the soil. There are pros and cons for doing both.

Perennial Meadow
You can buy a mat with pre-germinated perennial wildflowers in it, by the metre, which is reasonably expensive. However, once bought and installed, there is no more cost and very little maintenance from one year to the next, as no cutting or weeding is needed as the mat comes 'weed free'.

Vegetables
Decide whether you want to Grow From Seed or Buy Established Seedlings.
Growing from seed is inexpensive, takes time, and can have variable results. Buying seedlings is

comparatively expensive, takes no time, and has more chance of producing the hoped-for results. Vegetables grow best with regular care. They require good soil preparation in advance, protection from pests, diseases, and birds, feeding, and weeding.

Hedges

Decide how important the look of the hedges is in relation to the effort required to keep them looking neat, tidy and at the right height. Depending on the variety of plant used, hedges will require cutting once or possibly twice a year.

Leaves

Decide what you are going to do with the fallen leaves – compost or dispose.

- Decide whether you will invest in a leaf blower or rake.
- In the autumn, leaves need removing from all hard landscaped areas. The easiest thing to do is to compost them yourself, but for this to work well you will need a dedicated leaf compost bin. If you decide to bag them up and take them to the dump, it requires time and energy, but you do not use up valuable space.

The patio areas and the paths must be cleared of leaves. If left they will make these surfaces very slippery and difficult to use.

Leaves should not be allowed to stay on the lawn as they will block the light and create brown patches or baldness.

Leaves must be taken out of any water features, as they will clog up the pump and discolour the water. They will also contribute to the water becoming stagnant in the fullness of time.

Leaves should be raked off the driveway as it will spoil the look of the gravel, giving it a dirty appearance, and if the leaves are left to rot down, it will encourage weed growth.

To download a list of the most used Maintenance Actions required to keep your garden looking good, go to www.yorkshiregardendesigner.co.uk/Toolbox.

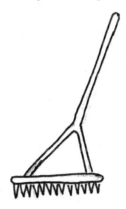

Chapter 5

Where to get Ideas and Inspiration from

If you are faced with a completely blank garden, or one you would like to change, now, and only now, is the right time to look for ideas and inspiration, and there are no shortage of places to look. There are books, magazines, the television, the radio, flower shows, art, sculpture, talks, clubs, the internet, open gardens (private individuals', privately owned estates, the National Garden Scheme – aka the Yellow Book gardens – the National Trust, English Heritage, the Royal Horticultural Society and more), parks, and the wider landscape about you. There is so much to choose from, now that you are on the lookout, it is very easy to become overwhelmed, side-tracked, or just do nothing.

Get Rid of Ideas That Do Not Apply to You

The good news is that you now know what you are looking for. You know what your Foundation List is made up of, what the Core Conditions are in your garden, and how much Core Maintenance Time you have got. Now it's much easier to make decisions about the garden, because every idea you think about or picture you look at, will go through the filtering process of the Three Foundation Steps. This approach will allow you to dismiss nearly 70% of the ideas you encounter within minutes (if not seconds) of looking at them – however attractive they are.

To give you an example, if your Foundation List includes a lawn, a vegetable garden with some nice herbaceous planting, a wildlife pond, and a bench with a view, and your Core Conditions are a small, north-facing garden, you can easily discount the notion of a summer house. This is because you have only got space for the bench and, as a north-facing garden doesn't get much sun, a summer house would be dark inside anyway. It doesn't matter how beautiful the summer house is, it does not fit in with the Foundation List and the Core Conditions, so there is no point wasting time considering one.

List all the ideas that fit in with your Foundation List and spend a little time considering each one. Divide the garden into major areas, then sort your ideas into those areas, being very careful to only keep those that truly answer requirements on your Foundation List.

What To Do With the Ideas That Make it Through the Three Step Process

Most sources of inspiration are images of gardens, as pictures in magazine, on the television, the internet etc. While you will have a huge selection to choose from, the downside is that you are outside the situation. This can make it more difficult to assess whether it's something for you to consider, because you are removed from the experience of it.

The way round this is to try to visualize the item or idea actually working in your garden and to find out what it feels like. The first thing to do is to define what it is in the picture you are attracted to. Is it a particular item of furniture, a focal point, or the way the planting has been done? Take one thing at a time and work out where it would go in your garden. If you have identified a style of planting in the picture as something you like, work out where the conditions are in your garden that those plants would thrive, using the information from your Core Conditions. Once you have done that, go outside and look at the area you have identified, and try to visualize those plants in that spot. Bring the picture with you if you can. Does it fit in with the surroundings? Would the planting obscure your neighbour's property or the beautiful view beyond? Where would you be sitting to enjoy the planting scheme? Does it feel like a garden should? How does it feel to you?

Pictures will trigger ideas and get you thinking. For example:

- You could see a particular plant you find really attractive, but having looked it up, you find that it will grow too tall for your garden. This could lead you to look at the rest of the genus to see if there is another plant within that family that still has the attractive elements you like but grows less quickly or to a smaller final height. The result is a plant you like, that will thrive in your garden without becoming a burden to you to look after.

- You could see a pond that gives you ideas for finishing the edges of the pond you are going to have.

- You could see a lawn of a particular shape that would be worth discussing.

- You could see plants in colour combinations you hadn't thought of or seen before.

- You could see clever ways to save space, water, and time - there is endless potential.

Experience is More Important

Wherever possible, go to an actual physical garden to experience it with all your senses, as it's much easier to gauge what you like by doing so in person. Whenever possible, be aware of your surroundings and walk around noticing what you find attractive and what you do not. It's much easier to recreate an experience because you can talk about it with passion and accuracy.

A couple of years ago, I decided to design a swing seat for my show garden at the Harrogate Spring Flower Show. This of course got me looking at other swing seats and tips online and in magazines for inspiration. Of the many I found online, one was by a company called Sitting Spiritually, who make lovely wooden seats with a sizeable price tag attached. The Flower Show came and went (I got a Gold medal, thankfully), and so I thought no more of Sitting Spiritually, until I attended the Chelsea Flower Show later that year. There I found Sitting Spiritually had a stand at the show and, because I'd been curious about how they justified their price tags, I got into conversation with its owner, Martyn Long. He invited me to sit on one of their seats. That was the point I *got* what they are all about and the value of the attention to detail that they apply to all their products.

The finish on the wood was so soft, luxurious, and smooth, that it was impossible not to keep stroking it. I also found that the way the seat had been hung made the experience of swinging in it a very comfortable one - unlike the one I had designed!

Now at least two of my clients have swing seats from Sitting Spiritually in their gardens, all because I actually experienced the product for myself and so could advise them. So I cannot emphasise enough how important it is to experience something wherever possible.

If you'd like to see the swing seats of Sitting Spiritually, go to www.sittingspiritually.co.uk. Better still, find one and sit on it!

There are interesting gardens to take inspiration from everywhere, so visit a few to get an idea how different gardeners handle the same issues you have in your own garden. Just because a garden is a big one and you have a small one, does not mean that you cannot find a good solution there - especially if, when you visit, you hold in your mind the particular issue you need to find solutions for.

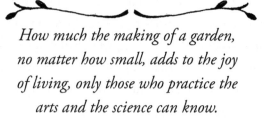

How much the making of a garden,
no matter how small, adds to the joy
of living, only those who practice the
arts and the science can know.

E. H. WILSON

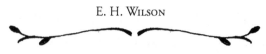

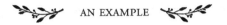 AN EXAMPLE

I was designing a garden that was quite exposed, which got more than its fair share of battering from the wind, so the planting plan had to take into account the cold, windy conditions. A group of plants that has adapted to deal with such conditions very successfully (amongst others) are the grass family, due to their reduced leaf surface and lack of rigid structure, so I wanted to see some grasses 'in action', so to speak.

Near to where I live is Scampston Hall and Garden, which boasts a Walled Garden that was redesigned in 1999 by the great designer and plantsman Piet Oudolf, who specialises in creating modern perennial meadows. He is credited with having brought the diversity of the grass family to the attention of the wider public, through his work, show gardens, and books. Scampston seemed the ideal place to go and see how an expert plantsman had used grasses, and perhaps find some ideas I could use myself. I was lucky it was late summer when I needed the ideas, as I think the gardens at Scampston look their best at this time, so there was lots to see on the day of my visit. I found great blocks of different grasses planted together with some of the tougher perennials interspersed throughout the blocks, which brought colour and texture to the whole picture. The message I took away that day was how effective blocks of grasses were, especially as I had almost always used single specimen grasses dotted throughout my planting schemes in the past. The resulting garden I designed was stunning to look at, easy to care for, and well able to cope with the physical conditions in the garden. If you'd like to see the gardens at Scampston, go to www.scampston.co.uk

The Game-Changing Question

It's very easy to get seduced and over-enthused by how pretty some of these gardens look, but the clincher question is, '**How long does it take to keep this garden looking like this?**' It is rare to see any comment made as to how long it takes to look after gardens, because they can take up huge amounts of time, as you probably know. The more they look as though they just 'happened' that way, the more time it has probably taken to achieve that specific effect.

It will probably amaze you, and totally change your perspective, if you ask the people who look after gardens professionally how long it has taken to create a particular bed or look. Having worked for English Heritage in Belsay Hall, Castle, and Garden, in Northumberland, I can tell you from personal experience that it takes hours and hours of work to keep seemly 'natural' looking beds at their best.

The same question should be applied to those beautiful pictures you see, although that will be a bit more difficult to work out, as it relies on your knowledge of gardening. The important thing is to hold this game-changing question in mind and not think you can just recreate the image 'just like that' in your own garden. In this way you will not be disappointed when the perfect result, as shown in the photo, does not happen quite as you would like it to.

Resources

Decide what medium of research you relate best to and start with that initially, but do not ignore other methods of research.

 Online

The Internet is an almost unlimited resource for ideas, with specialist lifestyle websites such as Pinterest (www.pinterest.com) and Houzz (www.houzz.co.uk) as good places to start. Pick an area of the garden and use that to choose keywords which you will use to start your search. Look for blogs and short videos on YouTube and do not forget to click on the Images tab to get pictures of your keywords. If you have got to grips with social media, Facebook and Twitter can be good ways of finding interesting people and groups with good ideas to investigate further.

Printed

Subscribe to the gardening magazines that have good illustrations, such as Gardeners' World, Gardens Illustrated, and The English Garden, to name but a few. You could also go to a news agent and flick through a few magazines till you find one with the types and styles of pictures you like. Cut out the pictures that attract you and think about them using the Three Foundation Steps as guides.

Television

Gardening programmes are great sources of inspiration and variety because you get to see the gardens in real time and in three dimensions (as far as is possible on a TV). Gardeners' World with Monty Don is interesting and there are many more, some with greater bias towards gardening tips and others to that of design. As these programmes come and go quite quickly, it is best to watch a few that are on at the time of you looking for ideas and then decide which one(s) are most interesting to you.

Radio

Gardeners Question Time on BBC Radio 4 is a programme based on random questions from the audience with answers from a panel of experts. The questions are very varied and I've often found the answers to be a source of inspiration and interest. There are also other programmes based on specific gardens or designers if you look for them.

Experiential

Spend time in actual gardens and get a feel for what is going on in them. It doesn't matter whether they are open professionally, occasionally, or privately, go and look at as many as possible. If you can, take lots of photos as a memory aid.

Show gardens are excellent sources of inspiration and good ideas. The jewel in the show garden crown is the Royal Horticultural Society's (RHS) Chelsea Flower Show, held in London every May and is well worth a visit. The RHS also run other flower shows in different parts of the country and at different times of the year, such as the Tatton Flower Show in Cheshire in July. For a full list of all RHS flower shows and locations, check their website (www. rhs.org.uk). The BBC run a huge gardening show every June in Birmingham, called BBC Gardeners'

World Live, and in addition, there are lots of local and regional shows to go to as well. Although the RHS and the BBC run some of the biggest flower shows, there are other independent show, such as the Harrogate Flower Show, which now attracts over 100,000 visitors a year, so keep your eyes open for what is happening in your area.

The National Garden Scheme (NGS) is a brilliant way of seeing real gardens, created and looked after by real people in a scale the average garden owner can relate to. Under the NGS, individuals open their gardens to the public for only one or two days a year, when the garden is looking at its best, to raise money for charity. The gardens are vetted in advance for good design and horticultural interest by the NGS and the details of those selected are published in what is known as the Yellow Book. The Yellow Book is widely available to buy through book shops, garden centres, and other outlets, which allows you to plan to visit gardens in your area on days that suit you. You can also visit their website for information (www.ngs.org.uk). Cream teas and plant sales are also often included, which is an added bonus. I think the gardens that are open under the NGS are one of the most delightful and convivial ways of getting ideas, because you will meet fellow enthusiasts doing exactly the same as you.

Professional gardens or those that are always open to the public have good ideas as well, but remember that these gardens have been designed on a bigger scale than you are likely to have at home – do not be put off by this. I've found that the best way of going about finding ideas from big gardens is to have a mental list of three things you need ideas for and attempt to look only for those three things.

If you want ideas for a traditionally styled garden or to see plant combinations on a big scale, then the National Trust and English Heritage have many properties all over the country that are open for visiting, as well many independently run gardens too. My personal favourites are Scampston Hall in North Yorkshire (www.scampston.co.uk) and the National Trust's Packwood House near Birmingham. The Royal Horticultural Society also have four wonderful gardens in different parts of the country, showing examples of planting in different conditions, all of which are open for visiting.

Not to be missed from this section of professionally run gardens are botanical gardens, and the United Kingdom is blessed with many. Although the focus of these gardens is plant-orientated they have still been well designed to display the plant collections and to allow for pleasant movement throughout, making them great places to visit for ideas.

*Anyone who keeps the ability to
see beauty never grows old*

FRANZ KAFKA

Summary

Enjoy this process and do not rush it as it's very easy
to be over-enthusiastic at this point. Analyse your efforts to see if there are any themes developing. In this
way you will begin to establish what you do and do
not like. The clearer you are in establishing your brief,
the better the garden will be in the end. Ask yourself
if you can see yourself in the gardens that you have
identified as attractive and if you can, try and imagine
what it would feel like to actually be in that garden.
Once you have found a few of these, you are well on
the way to finding the right ideas for your garden.

Make a list of your top five ideas.

Chapter 6

What To Do if Your Garden
Is Becoming a Burden

This chapter is for you if you like your garden, but it does not fit into your lifestyle as you'd like it to. If nothing changes and you fast-forward a couple of years, it will probably have become too much to look after, and you will have been overwhelmed by it. You are going to have to adapt it to fit in with you.

The first thing to do is assess the existing maintenance of your current garden. Take each area in turn and consider all the things you normally do – maintenance-wise – in that area. Write them down. Now consider all the things you *should* normally be doing, if you had the time. Add these things to your list. It's worth investing time in this, as this is the baseline you are going to use to work out what is working for you and what is not. The key to this exercise, and where the real gold dust lies, is to note down how much time it takes you, on average, to do each task.

Be as truthful as possible with yourself about how much enjoyment you get from looking after the garden. For some people, pottering about the garden always having something to do in it is their idea of heaven, for others, only some aspects of maintenance are enjoyable. Neither approach is right or wrong, but the way you approach it in your mind is crucial to what you do next.

Sleep on your findings and then make a decision as to whether anything in the garden could be different. If you do think a change of approach would be beneficial to the way the garden fits into your lifestyle, consider the alternatives given below.

Change the Look and Maintenance Approach of Your Perennial Borders

Instead of going for a traditionally ordered look to your border, which is achieved through weeding, staking, dead-heading, splitting, replanting, mulching, soil care, and watering, go for a more hands-off approach, which involves none of the above. You may be forgiven for thinking that this is a recipe for disaster but the plants will sort themselves out. Admittedly this will result in a much more informal look, but if the right plants are used, the effect can be as stunning as a traditionally managed border – just different.

A brilliant and very illustrative comparison of the two methods of maintenance was given recently by Colin Crosbie, who is the Garden Curator at the Royal Horticultural Society's Garden at Wisley. He described and compared the Mixed Beds at Wisley – comprising perennials and shrubs, which are managed traditionally – to the Glasshouse Beds, also in the same topographical area of Wisley, which are not. The Glasshouse Beds – made up entirely of perennials and grasses – were planned and planted by the Dutch plantsman Piet Oudolf, who has a very different approach to planning and maintaining borders, finding his inspiration from the way plant communities behave in the wild.

The Mixed Borders are weeded, staked, dead-headed, split weekly, mulched with an organic mulch every two or three years, and watered regularly throughout the growing season. The period of interest is from June to October, when they are cut back, leaving the border empty of interest until the following year.

The Glasshouse Beds, on the other hand, are mulched with 5cm of gravel every seven years and left pretty much to their own devices. They are not staked, watered or fed, and as a result the plants grow into each other, support each other, and develop excellent root systems which can deal with the fluctuations and vagaries of the UK weather. There is interest from June to January, especially during the winter, as the plants are left standing throughout, only being cut down in February – often with just a hedge trimmer. Colin Crosbie said that it takes eighty hours a week (May to September) to look after the Mixed Borders (remember, they are very large) with the most amount of time being spent on invisible staking. It takes the same number of people only twenty-five hours per week (May to September) to look after the Glasshouse Beds, which are *even larger* than the Mixed Borders.

If you can visit the RHS garden at Wisley, go and have a look for yourself.

Change the Type of Perennials You Use

To cut the amount of time you spend on perennial maintenance, predominantly that of staking, you must pick the right plants. These are plants that can hold their own, do not allow other plants to overwhelm them, and are able to survive windy, stormy weather without being battered. This means tall plants with stiff stems, which break easily in strong winds, such as delphiniums, are not suitable. Noel Kingsbury, author, lecturer, and plantsman (www.noelkingsbury.com), gives the following plants as examples of those that can maintain their own space in the border – Geranium x oxonianum and cultivars, Hostas, Geranium sylvaticum and cultivars, Acanthus mollis, Liriope muscari and cultivars, Miscanthus sinensis and cultivars, and Anemone japonica and cultivars (a cultivar is the horticultural jargon for 'variety'). It has to be said that these plants could also be called 'thugs', so you will have to balance the 'pros' and 'cons' about using them, but on the whole, plants that spread easily are the ones that take the least looking after.

Piet Oudolf uses a lot of grasses because they are ideally suited to windy places, and most clump up very nicely. He has written a number of excellent books about his approach to planting for those who would like to learn more. Piet has been commissioned to plan and plant many schemes around the world and his work in the UK can be seen at Scampston Hall and Gardens in North Yorkshire, Trentham Gardens in Staffordshire, RHS Garden Wisley in Woking, Pensthorpe Natural Park in Norfolk, Serpentine Gallery in London, and Bury Court in Surrey. See his website www.oudolf.com for examples of his work in other countries.

Plants to avoid when taking the minimal-maintenance approach are those that require work, which will vary slightly depending on the conditions in your garden. Other types of plants to avoid are those that get easily swamped by their neighbours, and need help from you in maintaining their position in the border. If you are having to liberate the same plant every year, weigh up why you have it, and it might be that it comes out.

Cut Down on the Amount of Perennial Planting and Maximize What You Do Have

Another option to consider is reducing the amount of perennial planting you have, and placing the borders you do think you can look after in the locations where you will get maximum enjoyment – this is usually near the patio and the seating areas. Locate the main view-points from the house, which would typically be from the most frequently-used rooms, so that you can carry on enjoying the borders when inside as well. The ideal situation would be to locate a border that is adjacent to a well-used place outside and that is easily seen from at least one of your principle windows inside.

If you have chosen to cut down on the areas of perennial planting, you are then in a much stronger position to decide whether you favour the bare soil approach, or a weed-suppressant membrane.

Weed Suppressant Membrane or Bare Soil?

A common option is to use a weed suppressant membrane to keep control of the weeds. The advantages of doing this is that 95% of the weeds you would have had to deal with on bare soil no longer have the opportunity to germinate or root, let alone become established. The disadvantage, however, is that the plants you do want to encourage are prevented from spreading as naturally as they'd like to, and you will have to use a mulch or top dressing to hide the membrane, and this can look a little artificial. The mulch will also require annual topping up, and the development of the plants can look a little stilted if not handled correctly. That said, there is a lot going for the 'plant through gravel' look, and you can create quite different and interesting effects, depending on the gravel chosen.

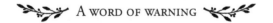 A WORD OF WARNING

Be very careful when choosing gravel if you are attracted by what is known as 'decorative aggregates', as it's very easy to get caught up in selecting a gravel that is too vivid for your garden and its surroundings. This is an easy mistake to make as you are looking at the gravel in isolation, with no plants or the wider landscape to give it context. In my opinion, gravel used for mulching should be 10mm in size and the least colourful option going, as it wants to blend in and complement the plants and the garden, not stand out in its own right.

Use More Shrubs and Less Perennials

Shrubs are a good choice when thinking about maintenance. They take much less time to look after and are better-suited to being planted through a weed suppressant membrane, without it looking odd, because of their habit and development. Some shrubs do require annual pruning to encourage flowers or fruit, but most will look their best if left to grow into their natural form, without pruning, provided the right sized plant has been chosen in the first place, to fit the available space.

Do not Be Too Precious About Your Lawn

If all the mowing sounds too much, there are several options for you to consider. Firstly, cut your lawn less often and let it grow a bit. As well as saving you time, it has the additional benefit of being better for the grass plants and the wildlife too.

Alternatively, just let the grass grow as it will and you will soon have a meadow to enjoy. You can add interest to the meadow by letting nature take its course over time. You could also start from scratch with either a meadow sown every year using annual seeds, such as was seen at the Olympic Park in 2012 or by doing something a little more sustainable by creating a perennial meadow by sowing seeds or using a pre-planted mat, which you unroll just like a carpet. All of these options look stunning in different ways.

A final option for you to consider is to not have a lawn at all.

There Is No Rule That Says the Whole Garden Needs To Be Cultivated

You could consider putting whole areas of the garden that you do not use often, or you can't see from the house, 'on hold', as there is no point is spending time and effort maintaining what no one sees or enjoys. This can be achieved by simply putting down a weed suppressant membrane with a top dressing of bark chips. If the area is far from the house and the places you sit and eat in when outside, you could let it become long grass and just let nature take its course.

That in itself could become a place of interest if you mow paths through it to allow access.

Take Out Areas That Are Time Consuming to Maintain

Take out features or areas that are difficult or time consuming to maintain, and replace them with things that are easier and/or quicker to look after. A recent client took out an old rockery, which had become infested with couch grass, and replaced it with lawn. Now he just mows the whole area quickly and easily. The removal of the weed infested, messy rockery, makes that part of the garden look and feel a much more pleasant place, so much so that he and his family now sit out there with pleasure.

Top Tips to Making Maintenance Easier

Whether you implement any of the alternatives given above or not, here are some tips to make looking after your garden easier.

 Make Sure Your Soil is Healthy

If your soil is healthy, you will know it, as your garden will be alive with plants and wildlife. If the soil is in poor condition your plants will either just sit there doing nothing, or die, so it is worth checking how healthy your soil is.

A healthy soil is made up of minerals (which provide structure), organic matter - such as bacteria, fungi, micro-organisms, insects, and invertebrates - and air and water. The water is vital because it transports nutrients to the roots of the plants and the presence of the air is essential as it supports the living organisms that cycle the nutrients and carbon required for life to exist.

The Worm Test

The presence of worms is an excellent indicator of the health of your soil. Dig a hole about a foot wide and a foot deep (30cm). Do not choose a day when the soil is frozen or very wet. Find somewhere that's easy to dig, if you have a choice. Place the soil from the hole on a plastic sheet and then count the number of earth worms you find in that sample. If you find five to eight, then your soil is in good condition, eight or more indicates your soil is in excellent health. Less than five indicates that your soil lacks health and fertility and that it would be beneficial to take action about it. The presence of no worms tells you that there is a lot of work ahead to rectify this sterile state.

Caring for your soil is straight forward and easy to do. For tips and techniques to revitalise your soil, visit:

www.yorkshiregardendesigner.co.uk/Toolbox

The Test for Poor/Good Drainage

Sometimes your soil might look and sound as though it does not drain well. But that tell-tale squelchy noise underfoot, and generally water-logged appearance, does not necessarily mean that you have a poorly drained soil, your soil may simply be compacted. Compacted soils are very common and there are lots of different causes of compaction. Most of them are man-made, but even grazing animals and rain, over time, will cause some compaction.

There is an easy way to find out about the drainage capacity of your soil. Dig a small hole and put a regular sized paper cup with the bottom cut out in the hole, until at least two thirds of the cup is below ground. Fill the cup with water, marking on the side where the water level is when full. Note where the water level is 1 hour later, and if the water has dropped by at least 3cm, then you know that your soil has reasonable drainage. If not, you either have a clay soil, or one that is compacted (or both), but either way, you know you have to do something with it to get the best results and to avoid wasting your money.

If you'd like to see what happened when I did this test on my garden soil, go to:

www.yorkshiregardendesigner.co.uk/Toolbox

Complete Garden Maintenance
'Little, Often and Regularly'

Plants grow whether you like it or not, and whether you are at home or not, so the key to easy maintenance and keeping on top of everything is to do a little bit, often. To make it even easier and less overwhelming, do it *regularly*. Big blitzes, or 'garden binging' as one client of mine put it, does not work. It will make you feel that there is too much to do, not enough time to do it, and still the weeds keep growing!

Check the Size of the Plant Before Planting It

Check the full size of the plant, preferably before buying it, but certainly before you plant it.

Of all the plants available for use in the garden, trees are the ones you should do the most research into before planting them. You are aiming to plant a tree that is appropriate in size for the space you want to put it in. That is to say, one whose mature height and spread is not going to overwhelm the available space. Above all you want to avoid having to cut it back on a regular basis, because it has got too big.

 A CLASSIC EXAMPLE

Eucalypti trees are often planted in flower arranging for their attractive juvenile foliage. A eucalyptus is an enormous tree when left to its own devices, but can be kept in control by cutting it back using a technique known as coppicing, every two to three years. If the coppicing is not carried out, the plant literally shoots skyward, incredibly quickly, because that is what it really wants to do. Every time the tree is coppiced, its root system becomes stronger, giving it an excellent 'engine' for rapid growth when not restricted. Within a few years, there is a 25m (80ft) tree to contend with, plus a bill of several hundred pounds to take it down.

It's O.K. to Not Pick All the Fallen Leaves Up

It's very easy to get into the mind-set that all fallen leaves must be picked up, but there are some areas where it is actually more beneficial, and much easier, not to pick them up at all. If you have a woodland garden or an area of shrubs and/or ground cover, the leaves will just rot down, and although they do not have many inherent nutrients to contribute to the soil at this stage of the year, they are invaluable for improving its structure.

Make Your Borders and Planted Areas Easily Accessible

Most planting spaces are wider or bigger than the reach of the average human arm, so put in cunningly placed stepping stones around your border. This way you can get round the bed to care for it without standing on the soil, which must be avoided wherever possible.

If you find you have no alternative but to stand on the soil, make sure you do it on a dry day. A good rule of thumb is that if the soil sticks to your footwear, then it is too wet to work it.

Once you have done what you need to do, work backwards and fork over the footprints you have left.

Use the Right Tools for the Job

Good garden tools are expensive *but* worth every penny. There is little more depressing than trying to cut something with an implement that is blunt, or having to make do with a tool that is not designed to do the job in hand.

Use the Right Technique

Knowing what to do in advance of doing the job cuts down on the time it takes to do it.

Summary

Be realistic about how you are coping with the garden and how much time it is taking. There are no right or wrong answers, but the degree of enjoyment you take from the garden is the motivating force to making it fit into your lifestyle.

Chapter 7

What To Do If Your Garden Is Already Out Of Control

Start Again.

I know what this feels like. For several years, before starting my business, I fooled myself into thinking I could keep on top of the weeds, as well as keep up with my busy life and that a few 'native' plants were beneficial to the wildlife. Then one day I looked at it with honest eyes and saw an out of control 'jungle'. Couch grass had infested the border, running in and out of the plants' roots, and convolvulus was suffocating anything it could – which was everything! The whole garden looked unattractive and felt overwhelming. The fence was old and rotting, the boundary hedge was overgrown by many feet, robbing the garden of light, and the small pond was dank and overgrown with common sedge. Brambles had invaded the end of the garden, and the lawn was more a moss-fest than anything else. All in all, not a nice place to be in, and very depressing to look at.

Action was clearly needed and this became the starting point for The Garden Equation.

If you and your garden are in the same position I found myself in, the first thing to do is to stop wasting energy on feeling embarrassed about it, or blaming yourself for the state it is in. The second thing you need to do is to get used to the idea that, if at all possible, you need to start again.

You and your garden need a clean slate.

For the sake of your garden – and your sanity – the only sensible option at this point is to take everything out and begin again. It took me at least six months to get used to the idea and another couple to actually get started on it, so do not be alarmed at the amount of time it might take you to make the decision. At first I wanted to keep all the plants to use again, but I realised I would also be keeping the couch grass and the convolvulus. Given that they were a large part of the reason I was having to take such drastic action this was the last thing I wanted! With reluctance, I put all the plants into the municipal green bin for the City of York Council to compost.

Progress brings momentum. Once the project got underway and it was possible to see a little improvement, it didn't feel too bad about getting rid of plants, and as the work progressed, it became enjoyable and fulfilling to see how much had been achieved.

With the garden cleared of everything except the trees and mature shrubs – it would have been too expensive to replace them, and taken too long for new ones to reach maturity – it became much easier to think about my garden. I was also able to stop mourning the wastage of my previous plants, because this had become an opportunity to try out new things. All in all, I found that beginning again was very liberating, which is why I wrote the process down. Since then I've always used this method – which I came to call The Garden Equation – in the gardens of my clients, with great success.

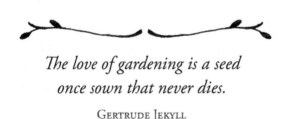

The love of gardening is a seed once sown that never dies.

GERTRUDE JEKYLL

The Options If You Have A Big Garden

The approach already described works well if you have got a small to medium sized garden and you can do it all in one go, but it becomes much more daunting if you have got a large garden. Of course there would be much less upheaval in the long run if you tackle the whole garden at once, but if you can't face this, or it costs too much to do in one go, I suggest that you divide the garden up into different areas. Start with the one that has the most impact on you, especially from inside the house. You can decide to do one area per year. Or perhaps, in order to fit the garden into your lifestyle, you might decide to apply some of the alternatives to traditional and time-consuming maintenance already discussed in Chapter 6, and NOT do some parts of the garden at all.

The Positive Power of a Fresh Start

At this point, you might be thinking of all the negative aspects that ripping everything out and starting again will bring. While you are not wrong that it will get worse before it gets better, starting again is one of the most powerful things you can do in terms of creating a garden that fits into your lifestyle. If any other options had been available, you would have likely taken them, so begin by accepting where you are at, and concentrate on the good outcome that will eventually come as a result of starting from scratch. While you may not see this immediately, you have one of the best advantages, because you are not influenced by anything except the boundaries, soil, orientation, weather and, possibly, a few mature trees or shrubs. This is the least possible number of factors that have to be taken into consideration when designing a garden. The lack of things to consider will bring you freedom to tailor the garden to fit perfectly into your lifestyle. No one gets to experience this unless they are doing what you are about to do.

To see some examples of the transformation that beginning from scratch can bring, take a look at some Before and After Photos. Go to:
www.yorkshiregardendesigner.co.uk/Ideas.

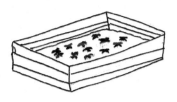

Chapter 8

The Next Steps:
How to Translate the Ideas and
Pretty Pictures into Reality

It is said that 'God is in the detail', and this is certainly the case when it comes to planning a garden – especially as you also have to factor in the passage of Time. It is at this stage that you need to decide whether you are going to design your garden yourself, or use a professional garden designer to take the project forward. The two options are quite different, so I will give the pros and cons for each.

The Pros and Cons of Using a Professional Garden Designer
On the 'Plus' side, you will save a lot of time, stress, and wasted money by utilising someone else's horti-

cultural expertise, creative flair, design training, and years of experience. You will be working in partnership with someone, rather than alone, and the margin for error during the build should be non-existent. A trained and experienced garden designer is also ideally placed to help make the right design decisions about the maintenance implications.

On the 'Minus' side a garden designer will cost money, as any expert would. Additionally, the success of the project is reliant on the strength and quality of the communication between you and your designer, and their ability to interpret your dreams. Hiring a designer also means you are not in complete control of the project.

Applying The Three Foundation Steps When Using A Garden Designer

This is a case of 'Forewarned is forearmed'. Although the process of designing a garden can vary widely, all professional garden designers should start the process with the first two Foundation Steps: clarify the experience you want from your garden, and find out what physical conditions there are to work with. However, very few garden designers think about the maintenance implications of the design like I do, at this stage of the process, so it is up to you to take responsibility for introducing the idea yourself to your designer.

If they are experienced (and I would hope that you have chosen to work with someone who is), they are ideally placed to advise you as to how much effort it should take to look after each area of the garden. Keep asking questions about every aspect of the garden as the design develops. This way the end result will be a garden that fits in with your lifestyle.

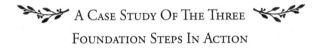

A CASE STUDY OF THE THREE FOUNDATION STEPS IN ACTION

In 2010, Edward and Jill were referred to me by a friend of theirs. They had sold the family home in a North York Moors village the previous year and bought a new, smaller townhouse in York. Their previous home had a large garden, but their new garden was smaller. They had settled in and wanted to get started on the garden.

Friends suggested that they get ideas from the local National Trust garden Edward volunteered in but he found he was overwhelmed by the quantity of nice ideas to choose from, and could not adjust to the scale of his own garden. Between them, Edward and Jill had a go but just ground to a halt because none of it felt or looked right to them.

The first thing we did together was to go through the three steps to establish their Core Information. This is the brief I wrote and worked from:

Step One: The Experience of the Garden

You love being outside and want the garden to be a place of tranquillity and beauty where you can potter about and relax. What you look at is a very important element of your lifestyle, so you want to be surrounded by beautiful, colourful planting within a strong structure. You like the calmness and simplicity of the symmetry, rhythm, and unity found in formal gardens.

Foundation List

- To eat outside in the sun
- A 'gin and tonic' bench
- Beautiful planting for late spring, summer, and autumn
- A symmetrical structure
- Access to the garage and outhouse
- To have a focal point using the decorative urn from previous house

Step Two: The Physical Conditions

The garden is on two levels facing east, which means it will get the morning sun at the end of the garden, and the evening sun about midway down the garden. The back of the house will be in shade due to adjacent buildings, except in the height of the summer, when the sun is high in the sky.

There are no privacy issues, but there is a tree at the end of the garden that needs to be removed as it is diseased. A new tree will be required in the same position to provide vertical interest and colour to the garden.

There are no features or existing planting to be accommodated as the garden is new and almost empty. There is a nice brick wall along the right hand side of the garden, which will be an ideal place for slightly tender climbers, as the wall will get a reasonable amount of sun.

The part of the garden nearest the house will probably be chillier than the far end, as the positioning of the garage will create a wind tunnel.

The soil is almost pure clay and quite compacted due to the building works.

Step 3: Maintenance Considerations

Edward and Jill loved being in the garden with things to do, so I anticipated them having quite a lot of time to look after it. At this stage, they estimated they would have between two and five hours a week, depending on the time of year. They enjoyed keeping the lawn mown, dead heading the flowering plants, weeding, staking, and tying plants in, so long as the quantity of work did not become a burden.

Interpretation

The garden that came about can be seen at: www.yorkshiregardendesigner.co.uk/Ideas/CaseStudy and it is entirely the result of the information identified in The Three Foundation Steps, with every one of the points in the Foundation List being incorporated.

Yorkshire Garden Designer created a formal, symmetrical shape for the paths in the lower part of the garden, which accommodated a table and chairs in the sunniest place, and access to the doors into the garage and outhouse, without seeming to do so in a contrived way. I used a planting bed to break up the space so that it didn't feel like a runway through to the steps, and used planting to soften the otherwise hard lines of the paving. The urn that had been brought from the previous house was put into a planting bed where it became the focal point of the lower part of the garden and is visible from the house as well.

The planting in the lower part of the garden was chosen specifically because of its ability to thrive in clay soil. The colours used are blues, pinks, purples, whites and silvers, and are at their peak in the early summer.

The upper garden is centred on a perfectly circular lawn, with a wide access path around it, which emphasises the shape for easy viewing from the house. The soil here is better drained so different plants, with a different colour palette, have been used. Here there are reds, yellows, oranges, whites, and blues, which flower later on into the year and grow taller. At the far end of the garden, there is the 'gin and tonic' bench, which gives the owners a different perspective on their house and garden, as well as enjoying the last of the evening sun.

The inspiration for this garden came from a visit to the formal gardens at Harewood House, West Yorkshire, where I saw how well a symmetrical pattern worked. Harewood House is, of course, on a much bigger scale, but while I was there I looked for a part of the pattern that might work in a smaller setting, and that got me thinking.

Applying The Three Foundation Steps can seem laborious at this stage, and there are moments when it would be tempting to give up, so bear in mind, 'Rome wasn't built in a day', and neither are the best gardens. Take your time and enjoy the illusion of being in control.

Cost, time, and effort are the deciding factors here, but whichever route you decide to take, the outcome will always be more successful because you now have the right information to make a meaningful and informed decision.

How to Hire a Garden Designer Who Knows Their Stuff

Garden design is an unregulated industry and anyone can be a garden designer, with no training whatsoever. Yet there are designers who have spent years learning about plants, where to plant them, how to design a usable space, and all the construction knowledge needed to do that. Many of them, like me, believe in the value to the client of professional organisations and have become Registered Members of associations such as the Society of Garden Designers and the British Association of Landscape Industries. Gaining membership status in these organisations happens by a tough adjudication process and it is frustrating to the garden design industry to see clients being taken in by people who have spent a few weeks at college and/or say they 'know a bit about plants', which is apparently qualification enough to design a garden. Unfortunately these clients end up paying the price twice: one in hard cash and again in having to live with the impact of a badly designed, poorly built, and ineffectively planted garden.

If you think it's expensive to hire a
professional to do the job,
wait until you hire an amateur.

RED ADAIR

Here are a few things you can do to make sure you get a professional designer of gardens:

- Ideally you want to use a designer that someone you know has recommended to you to because they have used them to create a lovely garden. If that's not possible, find a garden you like the look of in the neighbourhood and ask the owners who did it for them – no one minds talking about their beautiful garden!

- If you can't get a good recommendation, find the website for the national professional organizations mentioned earlier, who have a list of designers or contractors, all of whom have been tested and accredited to a certain standard of expertise, professionalism and experience. In the UK that is the Society of Garden Designers www.sgd.org.uk and BALI, the British Association of Landscape Industries www.bali.co.uk.

Check online for the professional organisation of other countries.

- Decide how you would like the relationship to be between you and the designer. Believe me, you *do* have a choice about this. You can be in complete control and have the designer do exactly what you ask. Alternatively, you can give total control to the designer. The way I have found works best is to develop a relationship based on trust, and work with the client in partnership. This way, both designer and client work together to arrive at decisions that are based on good communication and discussion.

- Look for experience and take references from previous clients. No professional designer will mind you asking for a couple of references and a good question to ask the referee is, "Would you use them again?". Find out if they are a member of any professional organisations and if they have any training, though this could be on the job or at college. Ask to see photos of previous gardens they completed and find out if they know about plants.

- Never base your decision as to which garden designer to use on *price* alone, because you get what you pay for. The important things to decide are: do you trust them, and do you feel the designer is on the same wave length as you?

It is the *rapport* between you that will make or break the success of your garden.

What to Pay For Garden Design

This is a tricky one. Especially as you can't go onto the Internet and do a comparative search to find out.

So what should you do? All designers do NOT deliver the same thing in the same way, so if you do feel that you can trust them to understand you and to deliver your hopes and dreams, then you have made the most important decision there is to make in the process.

At some point, you will receive their quote. A client once told me that she only ever bought items, or used services, that were 'reassuringly expensive', and that she was suspicious of people offering to do something for very little money. To many customers, a low price indicates either a low quality service or product, or that the person offering it has such little faith in either themselves, or the product or service on offer, that they do not believe it is worth more. If they do not believe in themselves, their products, and services, why should you have faith in them? To illustrate this point further, ask yourself, are you wearing the cheapest clothes you could find? Did you eat the least expensive food for lunch? The answer to that is, no, of course not. Most of us do not buy on price *alone* (that doesn't mean we don't take our budget into account), so do not judge the designer just on this basis. Finding the right designer is an intuitive thing based on many different aspects. Go with your instincts because what we DO buy on is trust.

What you should pay for garden design is based on a combination of how confident you are that the designer is capable of delivering what you want, the problems that they will be providing solutions to, and whether you trust them. If they are going to do something for you that you cannot do for yourself, or are not willing to learn about, if you know there is good two-way communication between you, and if your gut instinct is to trust them, then they are worth every penny they ask for.

To give you an idea of actual cost, a wise colleague of mine once said that a professional, experienced, and trained garden designer, does the same type of job as a professional, experienced, and trained architect. There is just as much potential outside as there is inside to make mistakes and waste money, so you should expect to pay the same rates to a garden designer as you would an architect, if you want the job doing right.

The Pros and Cons of Designing Your Own Garden

On the 'Plus' side, there is enormous satisfaction in doing it yourself. You will learn many new skills and you will have the joy of nurturing your project from start to finish. You will be in complete control and you will not be paying the consultancy fees associated with using an expert.

On the 'Minus' side, it will take up three times the amount of time you anticipate, you will have to learn the necessary skills on the job, it will be a trial and error process with all the costs associated with that, and you will not have the benefit of experience and contacts to call upon.

Using The Garden Equation to Design Your Own Garden

The Three Foundation Steps that make up The Garden Equation are your starting point, and everything you do and spend on the garden will stem from them. The first two are easier to apply and it can be quite difficult to keep the third Foundation Step in mind at this point. The important thing is to keep in mind that every aspect of the design will have a maintenance implication at all times.

If You Decide to Design Your Garden Yourself

This is not a lesson in how to design your own garden, but it will give you an idea of what is involved. You will need a scaled drawing of your garden to try out the main ideas and to find out how many square metres of space you have of the different types of planting or hand landscaping you will have to look after.

There are several ways of getting a scaled outline of your garden. You could have a go at measuring the garden yourself, using books or the Internet to learn how to do it. Remember to mark the doors and windows of the house, because you need to know where the views and access points are. Sketch on the features that allow you to do the things you identified in Foundation Step One. For example, if you like to eat outside with your family, create a patio for a table and chairs and either put it near the kitchen, for practical reasons, or in the sun/shade, depending on which one you prefer. If you like to read outside, decide whether you want to sit on a bench, a swing seat, or at a table. Then decide whether you want to sit in the shade or the sun and put an area of paving for the piece of furniture you like the most. Some of the best gardens have come about through the evolutionary process of trial and error, and there are some people who just seem to know where to put things and how they should look.

Another way of acquiring the outline of your garden is to buy a Planning Application map of your property from the Ordinance Survey (OS). These can be purchased from specialist suppliers (usually printers) or online. See www.ordnancesurvey.co.uk/resources/planning-application-maps.html for further details. This has the advantage of being to scale without you doing a survey. The downside is that the scale will be very large, so the outline of your actual garden will be very small. I suggest that you get the scale of the outline reduced, which will increase the size of the outline, making it easier to work on. This is, however, an additional service you need to ask for. In addition, in my experience OS do not always update their records, so if your home is within a new development, it is possible that the OS outline will not show the new boundaries. Nor will it show details like windows, doors, paths, or trees, so you still have to put them in before applying your Foundation List.

Once you have the structure of the garden sorted out, decide on the materials for the hard landscaping and then approach a good, reputable landscape contractor to discuss getting it built. To do the job properly, you will need more information than I have been able to briefly provide here. You can find this in books, online, or at local colleges.

Summary

There is a trade-off between time and money when it comes to deciding whether to design your own garden or to use a professional to help you. Only you can decide which is the more important one to base your decision on. Another way of looking at it is to decide which method would be more fun for you to be involved in. Whichever way you decide, the main thought to hold in your mind throughout the process is whether the option you choose fits comfortably into your lifestyle.

Part Two

Chapter 9

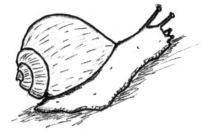

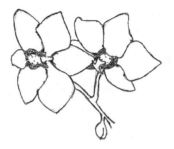

How to Keep the Garden in Tune with Your Lifestyle in the Future

To ensure your garden does not become a burden in the future, be more aware of how the time you have available to look after it fluctuates, up and down, with the consequential events in your life. Once you become aware of this, you will realise that your garden needs to change accordingly, as the amount of time you can spend on it fluctuates.

Often the changes in life happen gradually, but once you are aware the garden is becoming difficult to look after – for whatever reason – use The Three Foundation Steps to reassess the things that are important to you, in relation to being outside, and make small alterations to adapt the garden so that it remains manageable. Clues to look out for are when the words 'should' and 'ought to' start creeping into your vocabulary when you talk about looking after the garden. Another clue is when you put something off because the thought of it is just too much.

There are many things that will change how much time or motivation you have for the garden and it's important to recognise this. Your available time will go up or down depending on the circumstances you find yourself in. The garden must be adapted to fit in with you, to ensure that it does not become a burden. Gardens are not static things and neither are you. There is no point in trying to look after it if you do not have the time or ability to do so. It's also import-ant to remember that the garden is a living thing. It is changing all the time and you have to decide whether those changes fit in with you or not. There are lots of things that will affect how you enjoy the garden – the predictable ones and the not so predictable ones.

TOP TIP

Whenever something significant
causes a change for you,
your garden must change too.

The Predicable Sources of Change

Retirement usually brings lots more time to do the things you love, including gardening. I always think that retirement is the best time to have a new garden as most people have more time, lots of energy and enthusiasm, often combined with extensive horticultural knowledge and the money to have exactly what they want.

Retirement can also be the time for travel, and this can be planned for in advance, so that you do not come back to a jungle.

New jobs can result in less time for the garden, but sometimes it's the other way round. Often people's employment circumstances change and they start working from home. It's now very popular to have an outside office or studio, so the surrounding garden is an important part of that whole experience. When that happens, the time required to look after your garden is prioritised.

Care of grandchildren/children will inevitably change the demands on the garden and on the people who look after it. Rather than having to always restrict the activities of the children, which is exhausting and unsatisfactory, adapt the garden – or at least an area of it – so that you can relax when they are outside. Children require space to play in. Some of the plants need to be ball-proof, to avoid too much disappointment when play breaks the prized flower. It might also be sensible to incorporate various safety elements into the design, such as play bark instead of gravel or a fence round the pond, that would not otherwise be required, but you opt for all the same to give you peace of mind, which is the most important thing.

When possible, it's also good to plan for a change in circumstances in advance. I'm designing a garden for a couple, one of whom is ill and currently in remission. They love colour in abundance and want to get as much as possible into their garden by having a substantial area of perennial planting. Even at this stage, with only the plans in existence now, we all know that they will be taking those perennials out at some point and replacing them with lower maintenance shrubs, but they are determined to carry on enjoying the garden for as long as possible.

What To Do if Changes in Your Circumstances Are Significant But Short-Lived

If you know that something has changed for you, but it won't be forever, than it would be very wise to think about which bits of the garden can be left for the time being. Easy things to implement would include letting some of the lawn (or even all of it) grow long, and seeing what the grass will do when it's not cut once a week. You could also cover areas that are not easily seen from the house with a mulch or weed suppressant membrane, and just leave them. The goal here is to anticipate your lack of time for the garden and to build that into its management over the coming months.

Unpredictable Changes

Unfortunately, there are sad, unavoidable reasons – such as illness or bereavement – for the time spent on the garden being much reduced from normal. During these periods your garden can easily become a burden and get out of hand. At times like this, let the garden do its own thing without worrying about it until you want to go back to it. When this does happen, although the garden may look a terrible mess, it won't take too long to retrieve it, as you have already spent time getting the fundamentals right.

Using The Garden Equation To Keep Up With Change

I want you to think of The Garden Equation as a filter through which everything to do with the garden is assessed with. I'll show you an example:

You are given a voucher for the local garden centre which you decide to use as soon as possible. At the garden centre you see a plant with the most beautiful pink flower, which reminds you of one you had in a previous garden, so you decide to get it. In addition, it's on special offer so you would like to get two. At this point, I hope that you remember the Core Conditions in your garden. You know you have clay soil with a pH of seven and, unfortunately, the label on the plant in your hand tells you it's a rhododendron, which requires a soil with a pH of six or less in order for it to thrive and look beautiful. Hopefully you put the rhododendron back, albeit with regret, and look for something that will do well in the conditions in your garden. If you had decided to persevere with the rhododendron you would be spending time, money, and effort trying to get a plant to grow which is doomed to failure in the long run. That is time, money, and energy you might otherwise be spending elsewhere. So, buying the rhododendron does not fit in with two of the Core Conditions, and therefore should not be considered, however tempting…

Here is another example:

Your husband/wife has seen a wildlife pond in someone else's garden and would really like to have something similar in your garden. It clearly ticks the first of the Foundation Steps, in that it is something that would bring you pleasure. You then have to see if you have the right Core Conditions for a pond, which in an ideal situation would be in a place that was not overhung by trees. Assuming you do, you then have to assess how much Core Maintenance Time it will take to look after the pond over the whole year. Once you have made a decision about this, then you can realistically go ahead with putting the pond in without any fear that the garden will become too much.

On the other hand, if you find you are no longer able to look after a pond, it would be very beneficial to consider the benefits of getting it filled in, however drastic a move this might seem to you at the time.

Here are some things you can do to help you:

Have An Annual Review
Another way of staying aware of your garden is to have an annual review, usually in the autumn or over the winter. This will allow you to look back at the year that has just passed and assess whether anything has changed for you or not. Look at whether you managed the garden with ease in the previous year, or whether there were parts that had become more difficult to look after. At this point, have a discussion as to how to bring the garden back to being manageable and enjoyable for the following year. This is something I encourage previous clients to do as a matter of course, and whenever possible I recommend they include someone who can be objective and challenge the status quo.

Use the Right Tools

As I mentioned previously, selecting the right tools is essential. You do not want to waste time and energy improvising or 'making do'. The money you spend on getting the right tool or object will be more than repaid when you gain time for other things and enjoy the beauty of the garden.

I'm not suggesting that you have to buy the top of the range in everything, only that you should use tools that do the job. For example, if you need to prune a shrub, use secateurs that are sharp, strong enough to do the job without injuring you or breaking, with a blade that does not rust or chip. If you decide to stake a plant, use something that has been specifically designed to do that job, so you can install it effectively, quickly, and easily, and reuse it year after year. I regularly use several online companies, such as Harrod Horticultural Ltd. (www.harrodhorticultural. com) and Waitrose Garden (www.waitrosegarden. com) to find tools and equipment, and I have found that I have significantly reduced the time I take to do things in the garden when I've got the right tools.

Sometimes you find equipment in unlikely places, if you have got the eyes to see it, which is what happened with me when I bought what have become two of my most useful tools. At the time of purchase, I knew that if I didn't change something about the way

I was working, my back would become very painful in the future, so I had it in mind to do something but I wasn't sure what. As soon as I saw a seemingly well-made long handled spade and fork, I knew that they were the answer and I bought them on the spot. It didn't matter a bit that the shop I was in at the time was Aldi and I had gone in there to buy milk!

Five years later, they are still going strong.

Use the Internet

The third element to staying on top of things is to use the enormous wealth of information available on the Internet. When I first started learning about horticulture in college, we had to learn about every-thing – plant identification, gardening techniques, soil types, pH, pests, diseases, care etc. with weekly tests to ensure progress. Now I find that the most useful tool I have is not a particular reference book, but my smart phone, which gives me access to the wealth of information available on the Internet while I'm actually standing in the garden looking at the plant or situation in question. The Royal Horticul-tural Society have adapted their information pages for use on smartphones, so the information is available to gardeners quickly, easily and, most importantly, on the spot. Climate change and scientific research have brought about significant changes in the way various plants are now looked after and the array of new pests and diseases that are regularly being encountered means so much of what was taught in college when I was starting out is now obsolete anyway.

I also use the Internet to help me with looking after the garden. Lots of websites offer free advice about the garden in general, or about specific plants, so it really is quite easy to stay abreast of current practices and views about caring for it all.

A particular favourite of mine, which I recommend to all my clients, is Shoot Gardening (www.shoot-gardening.co.uk). You upload all the plants in your garden onto their website and it will send you monthly maintenance emails telling you exactly what to do and when. Instead of being overwhelmed by the enormity of the plant kingdom and all the skills needed to look after it, you get to learn about the specific plants in your garden, which is a great help when it comes to learning new things or gaining confidence in old ones. Shoot Gardening also has a wealth of 'How To' videos, addressing specific gardening techniques, such as pruning, so that when you are faced with a task you do not know how to do, you have an online resource to call upon without having to do time-consuming searches across the internet.

Keep Your Soil in Good Condition

It is vital to the success of the garden's future maintenance to understand the importance of looking after the soil, whether you are beginning with an empty space, a new space to you, or adapting an existing garden. The more time you spend on soil care, the easier it is to look after in the future and the less likely it is that your garden will become a mess and a burden.

The goal here is twofold. The first is to get rid of any compaction that exists in the soil of the planted areas. Building work inevitably creates compaction due to the nature of the work being carried out, the storage of materials, and the use of some types of machinery. It's also possible that there was existing compaction in the soil, which needs to be dealt with.

Get the soil dug over thoroughly, as deeply as is practical. It is quite common to find an old 'pan' of compacted soil just below the cultivation level from years ago, so check whether you have got one and get it broken through. It is also prudent to pay particular attention to the areas that had machinery or workmen on them.

Keep On Top of the Weeding

The second goal is to ensure the garden you create has the healthiest soil possible. This means it must be free from debris, unwanted plants, roots, and any other parts of a plant that might regrow in the future. You also want the soil to be of optimum health, fertility, and drainage, on the basis that there is nothing more soul-destroying than to be diligent about maintenance but not get the results your efforts should bring.

If you are starting with a new or empty garden, this process is not difficult, merely time consuming, but it is a little trickier if you are adapting an existing garden to fit in with your lifestyle. In such cases you will be working around the added impediment of existing plants. Weeds are survivors by their very nature, and will hide among the roots of the desired plants in order to escape detection.

If you are adapting your existing garden, for the first time, to fit in with the time you have got to look after it, I recommend that you make the additional effort and take the perennials and small shrubs that you want to keep out. Plant them in a temporary holding area elsewhere to give you some working space and prepare the border as you would a new garden. While the plants are out of the border you can take the opportunity to thoroughly clean their roots of any invading weed roots, and also split any of the perennials if necessary. If taking the plants out is not practical, due to their size or type, then do your best to attend to the soil around them. If you are preparing the soil among a lot of plants that cannot be taken out, then digging might cause more damage than good. In these circumstances do your best to alleviate any compaction using a fork, then apply a top dressing to introduce nutrients and soil structure. Let nature do the rest, but prepare yourself for the fact that more weeds will remain in the soil, which will take more of your time.

However time consuming and awkward the preparation of the soil is, it is worth persevering with it because it is unlikely you will get chance to have a good clean out again. Time spent on soil preparation will repay a hundred fold later, in terms of reduced time spent on weeding, and the development of a thriving garden.

Conclusion

This book focuses on a different way of thinking about your garden, and shows you how to change your rationale when it comes to your garden, in order to make it an integral part of your lifestyle. But in order to actually turn the ideas in The Garden Equation into an active reality, you need to have certain personal attributes, as well as theory.

At first, it will take *courage* to get the ball rolling. Once everything is underway, you will need *awareness* to maintain your changed approach to the garden. Finally, you need *persistent motivation* to make it all happen, especially if you decide not to seek professional help in turning the information you have gathered from The Three Foundation Steps into actual solid changes on the ground.

Rudyard Kipling put it very well in a quote I love from *Complete Verse*: 'Gardens are not made by singing 'Oh, how beautiful!' and sitting in the shade'.

If you feel daunted by the list of attributes I've given, then find someone who is enthusiastic, knowledgeable and interested to help you especially as it will take up your time, money, and energy to achieve all this. How do you know if The Garden Equation is working for you and your efforts are paying off?

If The Garden Equation is adding up correctly, the results will feel right. At a gut level, you will know instinctively that the decisions you have made are the right ones, because your garden will feel like a garden should to you. It will feel relaxed, comfortable, and enjoyable to be there. If it does not, then you know you have a bit more to do.

Tell Me About Your Garden

I am passionate about your garden and want you to enjoy it to the full. I would love to hear how you get on, so do please ring or email me with photos, questions, and your thoughts.

You can find out more about the garden design packages offered by Yorkshire Garden Designer by visiting my website at:
www.yorkshiregardendesigner.co.uk/Packages.

We offer fixed price bespoke garden design packages and garden design ideas consultancy.

If you would like to have a chat about any aspect of your garden, do please get in touch:

Email: sally@yorkshiregardendeisgner.co.uk

Telephone: +44 (0)1904 623 343

Or follow me on Social Media:

Blog: sign up via the website:
www.yorkshiregardendesigner.co.uk

Twitter: www.twitter.com/SallyTierney

Facebook:
www.facebook.com/YorkshireGardenDesigner

Sally Tierney

About The Author

Sally Tierney started her career in Garden Design in the middle of the night, twenty-one years ago, when the penny dropped that she loved helping people get the best out of their gardens.

After getting her degree in Landscape Management from The University of Leeds, and completing her Fine Gardening Apprenticeship with English Heritage, Sally started her company, Yorkshire Garden Designer. For the past 18 years, she has gone from strength to strength designing small- to medium-sized gardens across Yorkshire, gaining a Silver-Gilt medal at the Chelsea Flower Show and several Gold medals from the Harrogate Spring Flower Shows along the way.

Sally is passionate about delivering professional and manageable designs for the gardens she works on. She is a Registered Member of the Society of Garden Designers, and a Registered Designer with BALI (British Association of Landscape Industries). She lives in York, and although sadly is not a born and bred Yorkshire woman, has done the next best thing and produced two who are.